RELIGION AND MEDICINE

RELIGION AND MEDICINE

ESSAYS BY
MEMBERS OF THE METHODIST SOCIETY
FOR MEDICAL AND PASTORAL PSYCHOLOGY

Edited by
JOHN CROWLESMITH

WIPF & STOCK · Eugene, Oregon

Wipf and Stock Publishers
199 W 8th Ave, Suite 3
Eugene, OR 97401

Religion and Medicine
Essays by Members of the Methodist Society
for Medical and Pastoral Psychology
By Crowlesmith, John
Copyright©1962 Methodist Publishing - Epworth Press
ISBN 13: 978-1-5326-3826-8
Publication date 7/27/2017
Previously published by Epworth Press, 1962

Every effort has been made to trace the current
copyright owner of this publication but without success.
If you have any information or interest in the copyright,
please contact the publishers.

Preface

THE following Essays are, with one exception, written either by members of the Methodist Society for Medical and Pastoral Psychology, or by those who have lectured to the Society's Annual Conference and shared its discussions. The Society was founded in 1946 to draw together Ministers and Doctors within the Methodist Church for prayer, study and fellowship. It grew out of the Church's official Committee on Healing which was appointed by the Methodist Conference in 1937, and may be regarded as its practical application to the problems involved. Each contributor has been allowed freedom of expression, and must not necessarily be taken as expressing the views of the Committee on Healing. But, regarded as a whole, the book represents the findings of the M.S.M.P.P. over the past sixteen years as they have been worked out in conference in small groups meeting from time to time in various parts of the country. The field of what is known as 'Spiritual Healing' is at present greatly in need of exploration both from the medical and pastoral sides. Yet Doctors and Ministers are steadily coming to understand each other and are more and more working together to make Christian Healing, which includes both Medicine and Religion, a reality. These two disciplines should be partners in this enterprise, not rivals. It is our hope that what we have written may contribute in some measure to this end.

We of the Society would like especially to thank our 'Guest Writer', the Reverend Rupert E. Davies, for his willingness to help us in this collective attempt to express our conclusions. Also, to the Reverend William Strawson, who has lectured to us, but who is not a member of the Society, we would express our deep gratitude for his contribution. Our grateful thanks are given to Messrs. HOUGHTON MIFFLIN COMPANY of Boston, U.S.A. for their permission to include the extracts from Professor Carl Rogers' "Counseling and Psychotherapy" printed on pages 155-6. If any other quotations have been used throughout this book for which permission should have been sought and has not been, through inadvertence, we tender our humble apologies to authors and publishers alike.

JOHN CROWLESMITH

SIDMOUTH, DEVON
May 1962

Table of Contents

1. MEDICAL SCIENCE BEFORE CHRIST ... 1
   The Reverend Rupert E. Davies
   Methodist Minister, Tutor in Church History and the History of Christian Doctrine, Didsbury College, Bristol

2. NON-MEDICAL HEALING FROM THE AGE OF THE FATHERS TO THE EVANGELICAL REVIVAL ... 18
   The Reverend John Crowlesmith
   Methodist Minister. Secretary, the Methodist Church Committee on Healing, 1939–1960. Co-Secretary, the Methodist Society for Medical and Pastoral Psychology

3. PRESENT-DAY NON-MEDICAL METHODS OF HEALING ... 30
   The Reverend Leslie D. Weatherhead, C.B.E.
   Methodist Minister. Minister Emeritus, The City Temple. Co-President, Methodist Society for Medical and Pastoral Psychology

4. THE SIGNIFICANCE OF THE NEW TESTAMENT HEALING MIRACLES FOR THE MODERN HEALER ... 70
   The Reverend Erastus Evans
   Methodist Minister. Sometime Chairman of the Guild of Pastoral Psychology

5. THE THEOLOGY OF HEALING ... 90
   The Reverend William Strawson
   Methodist Minister. Tutor in Systematic Theology and Philosophy of Religion, Handsworth College, Birmingham

6. PRAYER AND HEALING ... 112
   The Reverend Ronald V. Spivey
   Methodist Minister. Associate Professor of Biblical Study, United Theological College, Bangalore

7. THE PSYCHOLOGY OF HEALING ... 125
   Doctor Percy L. Backus
   Co-President of the Methodist Society for Medical and Pastoral Psychology. Vice-Chairman of the Churches' Council of Healing

8 HEALING AND THE MINISTER   136
   The Reverend Reginald Brighton
   Methodist Minister. Member of the Methodist Committee on
   Healing. Member of the Committee of the Methodist Society
   for Medical and Pastoral Psychology. Member of the Executive
   Committee of the Churches' Council of Healing

9 THE DOCTOR AND HEALING   159
   Doctor Denis V. Martin
   Consultant Psychiatrist, Claybury Hospital, Essex

10 CO-OPERATION OF MINISTER AND DOCTOR   168
   The Reverend Lewis H. Allison
   Methodist Minister. Secretary, The Methodist Committee on
   Healing. Co-Secretary, The Methodist Society for Medical
   and Pastoral Psychology

   Doctor R. Paxton Graham
   Member of the Methodist Committee on Healing. Member
   of the Committee of the Methodist Society for Medical and
   Pastoral Psychology.

I
Medical Science before Christ
Rupert E. Davies

MEDICAL SCIENCE BEFORE CHRIST

IT IS IMPOSSIBLE to imagine a society which is not interested in disease and its cure. Even the most primitive members of the human race are distressed when their loved ones are in pain, and when they themselves are afflicted with an illness like the one which caused the death of someone they knew. If they hear of any foods or herbs or 'simples' which are reputed to have a curative effect, no doubt they use them hopefully, even if the use of them has to be secret. But, to a degree which still astonishes the modern investigator, primitive people take for granted many things which we conceive it to be our duty to fight against tooth and nail—death in childbirth, death from wounds, infant mortality, imbecility, dysentery, tuberculosis, and much more. These things are part of the established order; there is nothing to be done about them, for—if one should ask the reason why—the spirits that control the destinies of the tribe or society have so arranged the conditions of human life. And when something worse than the established order breaks out—a pestilence, the sudden illness or death of someone young and healthy, the unpredicted madness of someone thought wise and understanding—then this is a religious matter; the spirits have been offended, or have decided, for reasons of their own, to inflict an illness on an individual or a group. The priest or the man of magic is called in; he employs the traditional means of placating the angry divinities, and he may know some magical means of bending the spirits to his purpose (for it is of the essence of magic to mould the world according to one's will). Then, if he succeeds in his efforts, this is a sign of his knowledge of the will of heaven, and of the spirits' willingness to be appeased; if he fails, it is because the sin committed is too great or the spirits in this instance too obdurate.

In other words, in the simpler forms of human society, no distinction is made between the various parts of life; life is a unity, and religion embraces and permeates the whole. There is nothing which is particularly religious, but there is nothing which is outside religion. Similarly, there is no separation of the mind from the body, no special treatment for the one as distinct from the other;

each man is a unity, and the society to which he belongs is a unity. There is a sense in which the development of society, and of medicine, is the break-up of the primal unity of life—leading in the end, one may hope, to its ultimate re-unification on a higher level.

But our knowledge of all this is, of course, scanty and inferential, and the generalization which we have permitted ourselves may not be really allowable. We are on surer ground when we approach what the anthropologists call the 'higher primitive cultures'. Here we must select for our purpose the two main types which have influenced, indeed almost produced, our own civilization: the Semitic, covering many peoples in addition to the Hebrews, and the Hellenic, also taking many forms before it was crystallized into the civilization of Classical Greece. Both Semites and Greeks, as they emerged into that stage of cultures which is known to us from the earliest written records, inherited the conviction that illness is the result of sin, inflicted on mankind as a divine punishment. But they developed and modified this conviction in different ways.

Our best evidence of the Semitic attitude comes from the Assyrian inscriptions, dating from about 900 B.C. to about 600 B.C., and from the Old Testament. Since the Assyrians borrowed their language, their literature and their religion from the Babylonians, we may usually assume that what the Assyrians believed about medicine and religion the Babylonians also believed; and since there is little or no sign of development of thought on any subject, even warfare, during the great age of Assyrian power, we need not concern ourselves with working out the stages of Assyrian medical thought and practice. The characteristic idea of the Assyrians on the subject was not that disease was a divine punishment for sin—for this idea was common to all peoples at this period of history—but that disease *was* sin. It was the outward and visible sign of an inward and spiritual disgrace. The same word was in fact used both for sin and disease: '*shertu*'. If a man broke any of the myriad commandments of any of the gods or goddesses—whether it was Marduk, or Ea, or Ishtar, or Nin-Azu or Nin-karrak (the last two being especially concerned with the healing art)—and so was in a state of rebellion (even if he did not know it), he became at once spiritually impure; and at once he was liable to break out in spots, or internal ulcers, or demented acts. These symptoms of his impure state might be caused directly by the offended deity; or the deity might depart from the man, leaving him an easy prey to the demons that infested all parts of the atmosphere. But in either case his morbid state was the external sign of his inward defilement. Thus we have the prayer of a sick man: 'Impurity has befallen me. In order that thou mayest judge my case, in order that thou mayest pass judgement upon me, I have prostrated myself before thee. Judge my case: make thy decision concerning me; tear out the malignant disease from my body; destroy all evil in my flesh and in my muscles. Let the disease of my body, of my flesh, and of my muscles flee from me, and let me behold the light.' Was he suffering from rheumatoid arthritis?

Treatment followed the course indicated by this theory of disease. The priest was, of course, called in. He subjected the patient to a very long inquisition, similar, perhaps, to that conducted in the Confessionals of Catholic Christianity. 'Has he incited the father against the son? Has he incited the son against the father? Has he incited the friend against the friend? Has he said "Yes", when he ought to have said "No"? Has he used false scales?'—and so on through an interminable series of every possible moral and religious offence. If the patient at one or more points answered, 'Yes, I have'—and it seems difficult to see how he can have avoided doing so, if we grant that he wanted to be cured, and was therefore reasonably honest—all was then plain sailing: the appropriate rites of propitiation and, if necessary, exorcism, were proceeded with. But if the patient had nothing, absolutely nothing, on his conscience—and such people are met with even today—then it became necessary to discover what hidden, unconscious sin was causing the trouble. This could be done by inspecting the entrails of sacrificed animals, or by the interpretation of dreams. Once the illness was diagnosed, that is, once the sin was disclosed, the means of cure was easy to prescribe. What happened when the cure did not prove effective we are not told; no doubt the patient had failed to divulge his sin.

That the Assyrians had grasped the idea of unconscious sin is shown by what has just been described, and also by the fact that Assyrian priests were in the habit of performing an expiatory sacrifice on the eve of the great festivals to purify themselves in advance from any involuntary breach of ritual. Such a notion was useful for covering cases of apparently uncaused illness. But the more reflective Babylonians were not entirely satisfied with it, as we can see from the poem called *The Just Sick Man* (seventh century B.C.), where the sufferer cries out in despair: 'I have been likened to the man who has forgotten his august Lord, who has taken the name of God in vain. But I have devoted myself only to supplication, to prayer; prayer has been my rule of conduct; offerings, my law.' So perennial and universal is the problem posed by the Book of Job.

Thus for the Assyrians and Babylonians medical practice was the business of the priests. But, at least in Babylon, they did not have a complete monopoly. For the Code of Hammurabi, which may go back to 2000 B.C., lays down a rule of conduct and a scale of fees for medical men, though their function is not precisely described. It may be that they were principally employed in surgery, and corresponded to the surgical practitioners who, as we shall see, undoubtedly existed in Palestine in historical times.

The medical theory which emerges from the Old Testament is much the same as the one that we have found in Mesopotamia. The Hebrews, however, do not seem to have made the express identification of disease with sin that the Assyrians did, but simply to have regarded disease as the direct consequence of sin. It is therefore inflicted on man by God's direct action; 'I kill, and I make alive; I have wounded, and I heal' says God in Deuteronomy (32^{39}). When King Saul began to sink into melancholia, it was because 'the spirit of the LORD had departed from Saul, and an evil spirit from the LORD troubled him' (1 Samuel 14^{14}); and this visitation was due to Saul's sin in failing to exterminate the Amalekites at Samuel's behest. If God did not punish the sinner directly, His will was carried out by evil spirits, who were always ready to pounce on mankind. Thus madness resulted from the taking over of a man's body by a demon. A person so invaded had to be treated with great respect, since the demon might transfer his attentions to anyone who insulted him. Therefore the people in Israel who were most exempt from actual ill-treatment were 'prophets', who were inhabited by the spirit of God, and lunatics, who were inhabited by evil spirits. It has been suggested that many of the imprecatory Psalms are directed against demonic, not human enemies. In the preface to the Book of Job, it will be remembered, there is a variation on the usual divine procedure in causing disease; Satan, who in the book is God's servant, with the function of investigating human motives (and usually finding them unsatisfactory), is allowed by God to inflict on Job 'sore boils from the sole of his foot unto his crown' (Job 2^7), in order to test the sincerity of his piety—a very effective test, as it turned out.

When a man fell ill and did not quickly recover, his only resort was to the priest at the local sanctuary (it is interesting to speculate about the effect on the sickness and death rate produced by the enactment of 621 B.C., which destroyed all sanctuaries except the one in Jerusalem, and thus made it necessary for patients to undertake long journeys), unless he was lucky enough to know of a 'prophet' in the vicinity. A 'prophet' was thought to be more effective than the common or garden local priest—or at least some prophets were—as we can tell from the much greater frequency with which we hear of 'prophetic' cures than of 'priestly' cures. Elisha was the prime example of this, and he certainly had a wide reputation, reaching as far as Damascus (2 Kings 5^3). He was able to cure leprosy in one man and transfer it to another (2 Kings 5^{8-27}), to de-contaminate springs of water (2 Kings 2^{20}) and poisoned pottage (2 Kings 4^{41}), and to bring the dead back to life (2 Kings 4^{22-37}). There was more than a little of the 'witch-doctor' about Elisha. He did not content himself with prayer and invocation, but was an adept in magic as well; for it was by sympathetic magic, not artificial respiration, that the son of the Shunammite was revivified (2 Kings 4^{22-37}).

But preoccupation with divine causation did not entirely rule out purely human methods of treatment. We know that the 'balm of Gilead' (some kind of resinous gum), wormwood, gall-water (a brew of bitter herbs?), and the liver of various animals and fish were used for curative purposes. The best-known prescription in the Old Testament comes from Isaiah, acting perhaps at this point on a sub-prophetic level: 'Take a cake of figs. And they took and laid it on the boil' (2 Kings 20^7). The patient was King Hezekiah, and the 'cake' was presumably a poultice, which had the necessary effect on the king's boil. It is also clear that there was in existence a class of physicians, or at least of surgeons, in the period of the kings, and that they were not expected to do what lay within the medical province of the priest and prophet. In Isaiah 1^6 the prophet refers to the practice of squeezing a wound or sore, mollifying it with oil and binding it up, and does not suggest that this was a religious function. But the Chronicler is severely critical of King Asa, who was 'diseased in his feet; his disease was exceeding great: yet in his disease he sought not to the LORD, but to the physicians' (2 Chr 16^{12}). Yet whatever the priests said, the surgeons continued to exercise their skill on serious diseases. Among the many human skulls excavated at Lachish are three which have been trepanned, and the date of one at least of these operations is the eighth century B.C. In this case, we can tell that the patient survived the operation so successfully that new bone grew in the skull and the traces of the surgeon's saw were almost obliterated before the patient died. The imagination boggles at the painfulness of the operation.

The Hebrew attitude to disease survives all through the Old Testament period, and beyond it to the time of Christ—that is, far beyond the 'higher primitive' stage of Hebrew culture. On the face of it, it does not allow for much real development in theory or practice; there is no room for real diagnosis, or for the study of anatomy, more especially since it was a rigid rule that a dead body should not be tampered with. Yet there was one important element in it that held great promise for the future. This was the basic Hebrew conception of human personality. In order to grasp it we have to put right out of our heads the whole dualism of mind and body which has become a presupposition of European thinking. We have also to rid our minds of the idea of the soul as an entity separate, or at least separable, from the body. These notions are completely alien to Old Testament thought and religion. The Hebrew conceived man as a body animated by something which he called a *'nephesh'*. The normal translation of *'nephesh'* is 'soul', but this has so many false associations in modern thinking that it had better be abandoned as a translation. The word has a curious history; it meant at first 'neck' or 'throat'. The throat is the place where we can most clearly feel our breathing; and so *'nephesh'* came to mean 'breath'. Now the breath is the principle of life; so *'nephesh'* came to mean the 'principle of life', and this is its predominant meaning in Hebrew literature. Man, then, is a body animated by this 'principle of life', this *'nephesh'*; indeed, we can speak of man as a *'nephesh'*, and use the word *'nephesh'* in the place of the personal pronoun. Thus a man without *'nephesh'* is a corpse, and *'nephesh'* without a body is inconceivable. A living man is an indissoluble unity. There can be no 'immortality of the soul'; for there is no such thing as a soul, to the Hebrew way of thinking, and it is nonsense to talk of the immortality of the *'nephesh'*.

Another word, *'ruach'*, is sometimes used in place of *'nephesh'*. It originally means 'wind', and then 'breath', and then by a natural transition came to signify much the same as *'nephesh'*. But even in its original sense, and still more in its developed senses, *'ruach'* always has the connotation of *divine* inbreathing. The winds are the winds of *God*, the instruments of His purpose; the breath of a man comes from God, who alone gives life; and sometimes '*ruach*' comes from God to man with especial power and vehemence, so that he can do mighty deeds that only a man with this particular endowment, like Samson, could possibly do. But every man has his measure of '*ruach*'; and this gift of 'spirit' can be called either '*nephesh*' or '*ruach*'. Yet man is above everything a unity; we may not speak of body, soul, spirit, as three distinct parts of man; rather man is body, he is '*nephesh*', he is '*ruach*', according to the point of view from which we are looking at him. And this profound sense of the unity of man comes, perhaps, from the profound Hebrew sense of the unity of God.

It cannot be said that the ancient Hebrews made much use of this 'psychosomatic' view of man for healing purposes; but Jesus took it for granted, and acted upon it; and it lay ready for any degree of subsequent development.

The Greeks inherited from their past much the same view as the Assyrians and the Hebrews of disease as the divine punishment for sin, and for a long time there was no great difference to be observed in their development of the idea. This comes out very clearly in one of the main events of the *Iliad*, which reflects the beliefs of the Achaean period of Greek culture, to be dated somewhat after 1000 B.C. The Greeks before Troy were smitten by Phoebus Apollo with a dire and dreadful pestilence, the exact symptoms of which are never disclosed: 'The mules he (*sc.* Apollo) assailed first, and the swift dogs, but thereafter on the men themselves he let fly his stinging arrows, and smote; and ever did the pyres of the dead burn thick' (*Iliad*, I.50–2). Achilles, the leading warrior, called a public meeting of the assembled army to discover the cause of this serious setback to the Greeks' plans, and the truth was revealed by the seer, Calchas. Agamemnon, the generalissimo, had abducted the daughter of Chryses, the priest of Apollo, and therefore the god was fearfully angry: 'The god that smiteth afar has given woes, yea, and will give them, nor will he drive off the loathly pestilence from the Danaans, until we give back to her father the bright-eyed maiden, unbought, unransomed, and lead a sacred hecatomb to Chryse' (*Iliad*, I.97–100). This revelation aroused a stormy quarrel between Achilles and Agamemnon, since the latter proposed to take Briseis, Achilles' captive maiden, as a recompense for the loss of Chryseis, and Agamemnon's insistence on his proposal in despite of Achilles had serious consequences for the conduct of the war. But meanwhile Agamemnon gave up Chryseis; the army purified itself, the proper hecatombs were offered to Apollo, and the pestilence came to an end.

The *Odyssey*, somewhat later in time, reflects the same view of the cause of disease. We read of a 'father who lies in sickness, bearing grievous pains, a long while wasting away, and some cruel god assails him, but then to their (*sc.* his children's) joy the gods free him from his woe' (*Odyssey*, V.95–8). The sin which had caused the illness is not here mentioned, but is presupposed. So it is with the unfortunate Polyphemus, the Cyclopes, who has lost his single eye by the devices of Odysseus, and calls out for help to his brother Cyclopes. Odysseus has taken the precaution of telling Polyphemus that his name is Noman, and when the Cyclopes ask Polyphemus for the name of his assailant he gives it as Noman. So the Cyclopes answer: 'If then no man does violence to thee in thy loneliness, sickness which comes from great Zeus thou mayest in no wise escape. Nay, do thou pray to our father, the Lord Poseidon' (*Odyssey*, IX.410–13). Thus they were released from the obligation to come to the rescue of their comrade.

We may notice in the story of the Trojan pestilence a slight difference in the treatment of disease from what we have found among the Semitic peoples. The Assyrians, for whom sin *was* the disease, included close self-examination and repentance in the prescribed regimen, with sacrifices appended. The Hebrews resorted to prayer for recovery and sacrifices at the sanctuary. In other words, they thought that the relationship to God which had been impaired must be restored. The Greeks also were concerned to repair the broken relationship by sacrifices; but they also thought it necessary to 'purify themselves'. This purification, probably, took the form of a ceremonial ablution. They washed their bodies, not of course to make them physically clean, but to cleanse them from religious impurity. This practice is mentioned from time to time in Greek literature. Oedipus, in Sophocles' *Oedipus Tyrannus*, for instance, asks what purification he should carry out for the people of Thebes when an epidemic strikes the city. In this bodily purification may conceivably be found the germ of the great Greek doctors' attention to the physical side of a man in the treatment of disease. It may have been found that ceremonial ablutions, though purely religious in purpose, produced an excellent physical result as well; and the highly observant Greeks would not fail to act upon such a clue.

To the Greeks of Classical times Asclepius was the patron divinity of the healer's art. To Homer he was a mortal chieftain, who had learned the use of certain herbs from Cheiron, Achilles' tutor. Asclepius' son, Machaon, inherited his father's skill, and when Menelaus was wounded he 'sucked out his blood and cunningly spread thereon soothing drugs' (*Iliad*, IV.218). It was in later centuries that Asclepius was raised to the rank of a god, and we know that at least a hundred temples were dedicated to him. To these temples—and often to the temples of other divinities—resorted as many thousands of Greeks every year throughout the great period of Greek history, as, in proportion, find their way to Lourdes and the other great healing shrines of modern times. Round the ruins of the greatest of all Asclepius' temples, at Epidaurus, have been excavated the votive offerings which the grateful patients made to the god in return for their cure—tablets depicting the diseased part now cured, or written records of the internal pains from which deliverance has been granted.

The method of treatment was 'incubation'. Solemn rites, sometimes, no doubt, of a highly emotional character, took place in the temple in the evening, and rendered the invalids suitably suggestible. Then they all lay down—higgledy-piggledy, it would seem—on the floor of the temple, and slept, and dreamed the dreams which Asclepius designed for them. In these dreams the true nature of their illness was made known, and also the methods which should be taken for its cure; and if there was no cure, that fact was also made known—lest the god (and the priests) should be blamed for the patient's failure to recover. One of the commonest causes of application to the god was barrenness in women; if a child was born as the result of the measures suggested during the incubation, he was regarded as having been begotten by the god—though cynics were sometimes ready with another explanation. The 'prescriptions' which have survived are rarely of what we should call a medical nature; they must have operated chiefly by suggestion.

Very important in the whole procedure were the sacred snakes of Asclepius, though it is hard to discern their precise function. They were presumably snakes of a harmless kind, and were certainly tame; they were fed by virgin priestesses, and perhaps were exhibited to the patients before they went to sleep, or even while they slept, and were thought to help the appropriate dreams to come.[1] The snake was the symbol of the god, who was often pictured holding a rod with a snake entwined around it (the parallel to Moses and the priests of Egypt will at once spring to mind). It is quite possible that the Asclepius cult arose originally out of the worship of a sacred snake, with which Asclepius was later identified. We cannot doubt that here as elsewhere the snake, with its capacity for renewing its skin and its ability to live to a very great age, stood for the restoration of life and health in the mind of priest and patient; and Jung has much evidence in the cult of Asclepius for his view of the great healing significance of the serpent-symbol.

From modern excavations, rather than from ancient literature, we learn something further about the cures of Asclepius. His temple at Epidaurus is not very far from some healing springs; it is so situated as to provide easy opportunity for watching drama and for taking part in sports and gymnastics; and the air in the locality is pure and health-giving. We have hints, too, in our authorities, that diet and drugs played at least a small part in the curative process. Epidaurus, in fact, was a spa, as well as the centre of an enthusiastic worship. The relative contributions made to the cure of a patient by the 'natural' and the 'supernatural' means employed will be differently estimated by the modern student according to his presuppositions. But it may well be that the presumed effect of the 'natural' regimen was one of the incentives which turned Greek thinkers from theurgism to naturalism.

The chief instrument of this change, however, was the naturalistic philosophy of the 'Ionic' thinkers, from Thales of Miletus, who died in 546 B.C., to Heracleitus, who died at the end of the same century. These men turned all their attention to discovering the ultimate constituent, or constituents, of matter, and so arrived at a doctrine of 'nature' as something which underlies and explains all things. This teaching was the starting-point of all Western philosophic reflection, and was developed in many different ways. It has a definite bearing on the subject of our inquiry by positing something which was called the 'nature' of man, and leading men to investigate this 'nature' in the interests of healing, and finally to hold that healing consists in the restoration of this 'nature' which has been disturbed by illness or injury. First in the line of these 'physiologists' (the word means 'those who have

[1] Aristophanes, in a comic description in the *Plutus* of the proceedings, says that the snakes licked the patients.

studied nature') stands Alcmaeon of Croton in Sicily, a disciple of the great Pythagoras, and often called the 'Father of Greek medicine'. He flourished about 500 B.C. His writings are lost, but a later writer gives us a reliable account of his views: 'Alcmaeon states that health is maintained by the equilibrium of the physical qualities: the moist and the dry, the cold and the hot, the bitter and the sweet, and the others. The predominance of one of them causes disease. . . . Illness results, as far as its remote cause is concerned, from an excess of heat or of cold; as far as its immediate cause is concerned, from an excess or lack of nutriment; but in regard to its location, its seat is in the blood, or in the marrow, or in the brain. Sometimes ailments originate by virtue of external causes—as a result of the particular properties of the water of the region, or because of over-exertion, acts of violence, and similar causes. Health, on the other hand, consists in the well-balanced combination of the physical qualities'. No one can doubt that this attitude was the real foundation of what we call medical science.

So we come to the great Hippocrates, who was born in 460 B.C. on the Aegean island of Cos. He was one of the Asclepiadae, that is, he belonged to the guild of doctors which had already existed for some time on his native island and had taken the name of the god of healing. Sixty extant treatises bear his name; but not more than six are now thought to come from his hand, though all bear traces of his influence. He was a man of noble character, as well as supreme judgement and skill; he was learned and also humane, and one of the precepts attributed to him epitomizes his attitude to his work: 'Where the love of man is, there is also love of the Art.' His method consisted in patient, accurate observation of the sufferer, in a refusal to generalize until he was quite certain of his conclusions, and on the other hand in eagerness to use his assured results for the benefit of all his patients. He formulated many theories about disease, but his theories were always subordinate to his concern for the actual patient he was treating. His best-known genuine treatise is *Airs, Waters and Places*, and in a famous passage he expresses his conclusion about the apparent clash between theological and physiological theories of illness. He is discussing the effeminacy which was endemic among the Scythians, and which they themselves ascribed to the malign activity of a god: 'It appears to me that these affections are just as much divine as are all others, and that no disease is either more divine or more human than another, but that all are equally divine, for each of them has its own nature, and none of them arises without a natural cause.'

The spirit of Hippocrates is best summed up in his Oath, which may, indeed, be earlier in time than the master himself, but certainly expresses his conception of the physician's task: 'I swear by Apollo the physician and Asclepius and Hygieia and Panacaea, invoking all the gods and goddesses to be my witnesses, that I will fulfil this oath and this written covenant to the best of my power and of my judgement. I will look upon him who shall have taught me this art even as on mine own parents; I will share with him my substance, and supply his necessities if he be in need; I will regard his offspring even as my own brethren, and will teach them this art, if they desire to learn it, without fee or covenant. I will impart it by precept, by lecture and by all other manner of teaching, not only to my own sons but also to the sons of him who has taught me, and to disciples bound by covenant and oath according to the law of the physicians, but to none other. The regimen I adopt shall be for the benefit of the patients to the best of my power and judgement, not for their injury or for any wrongful purpose. I will not give a deadly drug to any one though it be asked of me, nor will I lead the way in such counsel; and likewise I will not give a woman a pessary to procure abortion. But I will keep my life and art in purity and holiness. Whatsoever house I enter, I will enter for the benefit of the sick, refraining from all voluntary wrongdoing and corruption, especially seduction of male or female, bond or free. Whatsoever things I hear or see concerning the life of men, in my attendance on the sick or even apart from my attendance, which ought not to be blabbed abroad, I will keep silence on them, counting such things to be as religious secrets. If I fulfil this oath and confound it not, be it mine to enjoy life and art alike, with good repute among all men for all time to come; but may the contrary befall me if I transgress and violate my oath.'

Hippocrates was the founder of a great school of doctors which survived for many centuries, and most of the writings ascribed to him were really written by members of this school. The Hippocratic corpus as a whole gives an illuminating picture of Greek medical practice at its best. We notice at once that anatomy and physiology were still largely unknown territory until they were explored by Alexandrian physicians in the third century B.C.; nor can we trace in the corpus any sign of a disciplined and orderly study of pathology. The general theory on which the Hippocratists worked was that health depended on the distribution of fire, earth, air and water within the body; these elements have the cardinal properties of dryness, warmth, coldness and moistness, and to the cardinal properties correspond the cardinal bodily fluids, blood, phlegm, yellow bile, and black bile. The basic necessity of life is 'innate heat', greatest in youth, and requiring the maximum fuel at that time, and gradually declining with age. There is also '*pneuma*', that is, 'spirit', circulating through the vessels of the body, and helping to keep it alive. When the 'innate heat' departs, man dies. But this theory did not prevent the doctors from making careful and accurate diagnoses, or from the recognition that nature itself is the best healer of disease.

Forty-two 'case-histories', mostly of patients who did not recover, survive in the Hippocratic collection, and this one, among many others, shows the carefulness of the doctor's observations: 'Her complaint began in the tongue; voice inarticulate; tongue red and parched. First day, shivered, then became heated. Third day, rigor, acute fever; reddish and hard swelling on both sides of neck and chest; extremities cold and livid; respiration elevated; drink returned by the nose; she could not swallow; alvine and urinary discharges suppressed. Fourth day, all symptoms exacerbated. Fifth day, she died.' The diagnosis was acute quinsy. No doubt it should have been diphtheria.

There is also a collection of 'aphorisms', any of which are still valid: 'Life is short, and the Art long; the opportunity fleeting; experiment dangerous, and judgement difficult. Yet we must be prepared not only to do our duty ourselves, but also patient, attendants and external circumstances must co-operate.' 'For extreme diseases, extreme methods of cure.' 'Sleep that puts an end to delirium is a good symptom.' 'The old have generally fewer complaints than the young; but those chronic diseases which do befall them generally never leave them.'

The Hippocratic physician was prepared to operate in extreme cases, and elaborate rules are laid down for the preparation of the operating theatre and behaviour therein. But his chief emphasis was on quiet and simple treatment, dietetics above all; his principles about food for the patient are widely accepted today: 'White meat is more digestible than dark', we are told, and water, barley water and lime water are strongly recommended in suitable cases. Baths, inunctions, clysters, warm and cold suffusions, massage, gymnastics and milder exercise, and the sparing use of drugs, complete the therapeutic methods of the Hippocratists. And in general we may claim for them that they advanced in medical practice to the very limit of what can be achieved by observation and induction, without dissection or experimental physiology and pathology, or the use of anaesthetics.

The modern critic might point out that for all their intelligence Hippocrates and his school gave little attention to mental factors in the causation of disease. Yet this point was not entirely overlooked by all the Greeks. Plato, in a passage from the *Charmides*, even seems to give a hint of the possibility of psychiatry. In this dialogue a Thracian disciple of a certain Zalmoxis agrees with the Greek physicians who say that it is not possible to cure the eyes without treating the head, or the head without treating the body as a whole, and adds that Zalmoxis holds that 'you should not treat the body without treating the soul; and this was no doubt the reason why most maladies could not be healed by the physicians of Greece—because they neglect the whole, on which they ought to spend their pains, for if this were out of order, it would be impossible for any one part to be in order. For all that is good and evil in the body and in man altogether is sprung from the soul and, flows along from thence, as it does from the head into the eyes. Wherefore the soul is to be treated first and foremost, if all was to be well with the head and the rest of the body. And the treatment of the soul, my good friend, is by means of certain charms, and these charms are words of the right sort. By the use of such words is self-control engendered in the soul, and as soon as it is engendered and present one may easily secure health to the head, and to the rest of the body also.' But this suggestion was not really followed up by the Greeks.

The conquests of Alexander the Great in the fourth century B.C. shifted the centre of Greek culture from the mainland of Greece to Alexandria. Here in the third and second centuries B.C. a school of medicine was organized, and here the first systematic study of anatomy took place. The greatest names are those of Erasistratus and Herophilus, but little of their work has survived. We know something, however, of Herophilus' account of the nervous system: he saw the membranes which cover the brain, and distinguished the cerebrum and the cerebellum; he also knew of the ventricles of the brain, the cranial and spinal nerves, the nerves of the heart and the coats of the eye; he gave its present name to the duodenum. Erasistratus seems to have distinguished very clearly the motor and sensory nerves. In general the Alexandrians made considerable advances in medical efficiency, without in any way improving on the spirit and attitude of the Hippocratists.

The medical knowledge available at the end of the first century B.C. was collected into one volume by Celsus, whose work has come down to us. Among the advances on Hippocratic practice, and on the practice of the early Alexandrians, which he records, are methods of tooth extraction and the wiring of teeth, and the procedure for tonsilectomy. The spirit and temper of the book shows that medical science among its best theorists and practitioners still retained a lofty conception of its ethical implications. Unfortunately we know that at the time at which Celsus wrote the Graeco-Roman world was full of quacks who traded on the ignorance and fears of the populace. It did not occur even to the Alexandrians to establish any diploma in medical knowledge, or, if it did, they held that the power to enforce it was lacking.

The history of pre-Christian medicine reaches its end and consummation in Galen, the most prolific of all the medical writers of antiquity. He died about A.D. 200, and so he overlaps the early history of Christianity, but he was not himself a Christian. His books cover anatomy, physiology, pathology, medical theory, therapeutics, clinical medicine and surgery—and include endless philosophizings and moralizings which were very much to the taste of the Christians and Muslims who later 'adopted' him. He knew everything that could be known on the subjects he treated, and knew that he was right on every disputed issue; it has been well said of him that he loved truth, but argument just as much. He had a vast practice in Rome, and had amassed the accumulated knowledge of all the schools of medicine. He really did believe in experiment, he had a good knowledge of the human skeleton, and he spent much labour on the dissection of animals. He does not mark the beginning of a new era in the history of human knowledge, for all his learning and intelligence; on the contrary he brings an age to its end. After the time of Galen medical science made virtually no advances until the Renaissance, for he was regarded as the epitome of all possible knowledge.

Christianity, in fact, took over the achievements of the Greeks too whole-heartedly. For all its greatness, Greek medicine was limited in its success by too sharp a division between soul and body, as Plato, unheeded, had pointed out. It needed to be corrected by the Hebrew conception of the wholeness of the human personality, and to be complemented by the respect of Jesus for every human person as a person—quite apart from the need to develop the experimental method far beyond what was possible for the Greeks. Some of these defects were put right in the Renaissance and afterwards; some of them still await correction.

2

*Non-Medical Healing
from the Age of the Fathers
to the
Evangelical Revival*

John Crowlesmith

NON-MEDICAL HEALING FROM THE AGE OF THE FATHERS TO THE EVANGELICAL REVIVAL

THE HISTORY of non-physical healing in the Christian Church is difficult to trace between apostolic and modern times. The age of the Fathers is well documented; we have a clear picture of Christian healing practices at that period. But after the sixth century the stream runs underground and only occasionally comes up to the surface. Not until we reach the revival of 'spiritual' or 'divine' healing in our own day, is there much to be gathered beyond occasional hints and glimpses.

The first three hundred years of Church history afford many instances of what went on in this particular field. Jewish religious thinking had seen a connection between sin and disease. Since the early Church was closely allied with Judaism, much of this concept was carried into patristic approaches, and inevitably coloured the treatment of sickness. Sin broke the necessary communion of man with God and interrupted the flow of divine health into his soul. Thus he became ill, but his illness, while manifesting itself on the physical plane, was, in reality, a spiritual defect.

One has only to glance through the Apocryphal Gospels to see that in this age Christianity was almost automatically equated with physical healing. If the Church really was, as St Paul had suggested, 'the body of Christ', then it could surely do in the world what Christ Himself had done in the flesh. Contrary to that of the Arians, Catholic theology proclaimed that even divinity itself was not complete without the flesh. Therefore the body was something to be maintained in perfect health, asceticism only being acceptable when the flesh had been given up to sin.

The Fathers differed about whether suffering was sent from God, but post baptismal disease was regarded as an indication that all was not well with the sufferer's soul. On the contrary, it was widely believed that it was the martyrs' profound experience of Christ that helped them to withstand the tortures of the arena. Similarly, it is significant that the Church at this time was specially successful in the treatment of mental illness. Incubation was practised in some basilicas, though on a diminishing scale. It is clear that body and soul were believed to be inter-related, each affecting the other. The Shepherd of Hermas cries passionately that to defile the body is to defile at the same time the Holy Spirit.[1] If that happens, he declares, it is impossible to go on living. Later, Cyprian sought to show how the life of the soul affected the nerves of the body, strengthening them so supernaturally that they could endure suffering without flinching.[2] It should be added that all through this period it was devoutly believed that reception of Holy Communion nourished the body as well as the soul, building both up together into one healthy personality. The Ante Nicene Church spoke of the Sacraments as 'the medicine of life', a phrase perhaps borrowed from the pagan mysteries, but one which must be taken as applying to the whole man.

Healings took different forms and were accomplished in different ways. Prayer, invocation of the Lord's Name, signing the sufferer with the Cross, exorcism, the laying on of hands and anointing with oil were all practised. At times insufflation seems to have been used, but only rarely. Clergy paid solemn visits to the homes of the sick, believing that just as the very shadow of Peter in Acts had had healing power, so would theirs. The Canons of Hippolytus[3] go so far as to say that if a bishop pays a moment's visit to a sick man's house, the sufferer will surely be healed. There was, inevitably, much of pagan magic associated with all this, especially when people took to wearing the Host round their necks as a charm, or keeping it in the house to ward off illness. But underneath everything there was a real belief in the power of Christ to heal.

There was, of course, much belief in demons, implied by the wide prevalence of the rites of exorcism. Evil was personalized in this way and given a local habitation and a name. Demons, so it was thought, entered not only the bodies of men but also those of animals, causing sickness, and could only be driven out by the proper exorcisms, pronounced in Christian circles in the name of the Church.

But of all the methods God used in healing, unction and the practice of laying on of hands were deemed the most efficacious.

---

[1] Book III, Similitude 5.
[2] Epistle xxxiii.
[3] *Canons of Hippolytus*, No. 199.

Anointing with oil dates from very early times in the Christian Church and has been carried on to our own day. There were special consecration prayers used in blessing the 'oil of the sick', the ceremony being conducted at first by either bishop or presbyter as the case might be. But the bishop was officially the fount of healing, so gradually the right of such consecration was restricted to him. Apparently, the sick were often brought to the church on litters, there to be anointed. Unction was believed to open the way for the return of the Holy Spirit, Whom the sick man had obviously lost by reason of the sin which must have caused the disease. Yet there must have been many instances of private anointing both in East and West. The *Sacramentary of Serapion*, an eleventh-century manuscript ascribed to Serapion, bishop of Thmuis, in the Thebais, about A.D. 350, says that people brought oil for the bishop to bless during the celebration of Holy Communion. This was also done at Rome in the third century. Such anointing was believed to cure both the disease of the soul and that of the body, restoring the patient to complete wholeness.

The gift of healing might be possessed by any Christian, even a layman. But if so, it was interpreted as a sign that he ought to be ordained and was worthy of the ministerial office. Generally, the healing power of the Church was believed to be mediated through the clergy. The bishop and his presbyters not only held healing services, but visited the sick at home, not to give medical treatment, but to bless the physician's medicine and the ordinary food of the household. There even seem to have been occasions when church choirs sang the offices in a sick-room.

Thus in the first years after the Apostolic age the Church practised healing in the name of Jesus Christ the Lord. Though undoubtedly at times, especially in common and vulgar use, there must have been a touch of magical superstition about it, yet there was a profound difference between pagan and Christian healing. The old heathen practices left the man, morally, substantially as he was before healing occurred; they did not change his way of life. In the Christian Church, the renewed presence of the Holy Spirit was evidenced by an ethical standard which banished sin and gave itself to goodness. Healing in the Christian faith was linked to purity of life. This is not to say that there were not individuals who fell short of this high ideal. But generally speaking, it was true that so much was expected of those who had claimed to be cured by the Church's rites.

Yet this state of affairs was not to endure for long. Disreputable quacks began to hide themselves in the cover of the Church. The spiritual life of the Church after the conversion of Constantine diminished. There were increasing heresies, disorder and divisions. Slowly, healing moved from the centre of the Church's practice to the circumference. Nursing and invalid care took the place of direct cure. Gregory Thaumaturgos, a contemporary of Cyprian, had many cases of immediate healing associated with his name, but there were few such after him. After the fourth century healing by prayer and purely spiritual means falls into the background, and the emphasis turns on hospitals and treatment centres, travelling from the inside to the outside. Although the institution of hospitals is not of Christian origin, it is true that the Church gave it a much deeper emphasis and a more central place in the life of the community. Justin Martyr tells us that quite early Christians accepted the responsibility of caring for their sick brethren and did it at their own expense. Deacons and deaconesses went to see them in their own homes. It was nothing unusual for rich and leisured women to spend their time in helping afflicted people in the name of Christ. Houses were opened in which poor sufferers could be treated by medical care. All this far-flung network of welfare work was in operation by the end of the fourth century. Bishop Eustathius appointed the presbyter Aerius to be director of the hospital at Sebaste in Pontus about the year A.D. 350.[4] Even Julian the Apostate had to admit that 'these impious Galileans give themselves to this kind of humanity'.[5] In Caesarea Basil built a hospital about A.D. 369 which was staffed by the most expert doctors and nurses of the time, and which became known far and wide for its treatment of leprosy. These establishments were one and all kept going by the generosity of Christian people and were not run for profit. But they differed from the earlier practice in that they made full use of all available professional medical knowledge.

There is no doubt that the barbarian invasions that finally led to the break up of the Roman Empire deeply divided and distressed the Church. It was hard to keep the deposit of the Faith untouched in the confusion and distress of the times. The emphasis on faith-healing present both in the Gospels and the practice of

[4] Epiphanius, *Haeres*, 75, Ch. 1.
[5] Fragment, p. 305 (Rheinwald), quoted by Dawson, *Healing: Pagan and Christian*, p. 157.

the Apostles and Fathers died away, and was replaced in the Dark Ages by healing from charms, amulets and relics, or from attendance at sacred sites and wells. It came to be believed that the mere pronouncing of the sacred name of Jesus was a sufficient cure for all ills. In this paganism had infiltrated into Christian Faith, since 'Name magic' was widely inherent in heathen occult practices. Even so great a mind as Origen[6] was touched by it and declared that the results of exorcism pronounced in the Name of Jesus need have no connection with our Lord Himself. So long as the letters of the Name were put in the right order, it had curative value. If that were so in his day, it can be assumed with some probability that it would be even more so as the Church entered the twilight period of a decreased theological and intellectual life.

It was not till A.D. 794 that England saw a hospital, and then it was at St Albans at a site directly connected with a famous saint and martyr. As monasteries grew, so they tended, as at St Gall in A.D. 820, to build infirmaries for the care of the sick. Out of these grew the great nursing fraternities of medieval times. The intercession and mediating activities of the saints took the place of the direct action of the Saviour. Often the saints themselves were believed to be healers and there are many traditions to that effect. St Martin in Gaul is said to have cured Paulinus of an affection of the eyes. St Veronica's handkerchief was believed to work miraculous healings, and cures were said to have been wrought at Glastonbury by the image of Joseph of Arimathea. St Blaise of Dalmatia laid hands on a child who was choking because of a bone in the throat and he was cured. Bede declares that people who drank water from the ground where the body of Oswald, the seventh-century King of Northumbria, had fallen in battle were cured of their sicknesses. When a sister of King Eegfrith lost the use of her legs and had to crawl on the ground, St Cuthbert sent her a linen girdle which cured her in three days. St David is said to have purified the poisonous waters at Bath. So the stories grew and multiplied in a non-critical, unhistorical age. Yet beneath them there may have been a stratum of reality. Suggestibility and deep religious faith will accomplish many things, and certainly predispose towards healing. The purity of the primitive practice had gone. Thaumaturgy came to take its place. But within it, it may well be that Christ still cured, and that not all was superstition and legend.

[6] *Contra Celsum*, I.24, 25.

During the Middle Ages, healing of the kind we are considering attached itself mainly to relics and shrines. The former, pilgrims returning from the Holy Land brought back, and, genuine or not, sold them to eager purchasers. So many pieces of the True Cross were venerated in Europe as would have made many crosses on which the Saviour of men might have died. The veneration of relics sprang from the Church's emphasis on the resurrection of the body. Ephrem the Syrian,[7] for example, urged that both soul and body were made for the resurrection and strongly supported the cult of saints' bones. Christians believed very vividly that the sainted dead, like all others who died 'in Christ', were, in fact, still alive and able to help those yet living in this world by their prayers. Objects that had been associated with them, if connected with prayer and devotion, had power to bring down upon the suppliant the power of God. Manichaean dualism still further increased the importance given to such things, since Mani taught that the body was evil and adopted a negative attitude towards it. The emphasis on relics in the Christian view of the time led strongly in the other direction. Soon no church was thought of as being really complete unless it possessed relics of a saint, and at times unseemly struggles took place over them. The Second Council of Nicea in A.D. 787 even made the consecration of a church obligatory on having them under the altar. St Augustine spoke of the relics of St Stephen at Hippo and gave accounts of blindness and other diseases being cured through flowers which had touched them. In the same way charms and amulets were believed to render their wearers invulnerable to disease. The Patriarch Nicephorus speaks of gold and silver crosses being worn, often containing pictures of incidents in the life of Christ, which assured life and health both for soul and body. We are told that Gregory of Tours wore such a cross and regularly changed the relic it contained. The lives of the saints are full of miracles of healing wrought in this way. Unfortunately these practices became widespread among Christians in spite of being continually preached against by Church leaders. The disease was believed to flee when something sacred touched the afflicted body. Effigies of diseased limbs that had been cured were hung up in the churches.

Needless to say, doubtful and superstitious practices attached themselves to such cults and usages. Jerome tells the story of a Christian jockey who protected his horses against enemy charms by

[7] *Carmine Nisibena*, xlii–li.

giving them water from the pitcher of St Hilarion. By using relics in this way one could wish all kinds of disease upon one's enemy. All this presents to the modern mind a picture of debased and futile superstition. If St Benedict were able to cause a vessel containing poison to fly into pieces just by making the sign of the Cross over it, then surely still more wonderful things could be wrought by the Holy Sacraments! Thus Augustine declared that a doctor lost his gout at baptism, and so did an actor his paralysis. Even the water in which a priest washed his hands after Mass was a cure for disease. Could, we are tempted to say, superstition go farther? Has the healing of Jesus so powerfully portrayed in the Gospels come to this?

At a slightly higher level of spirituality was the practice of visiting a sacred shrine in order to obtain healing. St Chad was the patron saint of many healing wells, the origin of whose sacredness goes far back beyond Christian times. Some of the waters undoubtedly had medicinal properties and were recommended by the medical profession, but many were thought to be healing-centres in their own right. Sir John Shorne, who was Rector of Marston, Bucks, from 1290 to 1314, is said to have healed diseases simply by prayer. But a well near was supposed to have come when, in a summer of excessive drought, he struck the ground with his staff. After his death pilgrims came to the well from all over the land, since it was thought to have healing powers, notably for ague and gout. Notable shrines visited for healing were those of John of Beverley and Thomas à Becket at Canterbury. St Hugh of Lincoln was so popular in this respect that after he was canonized in 1220 it became necessary to enlarge the church to accommodate the pilgrims. Even men like Simon de Montfort achieved a cult after their death. His tomb became a place of pilgrimage to which sick people came for healing for many years. Fifty-eight years after the Battle of Evesham, Edward II complained bitterly that de Montfort was still honoured in this way. St James of Compostella and the replica of the house at Nazareth built at Walsingham by Richeldis de Faverches, a pious and wealthy widow, drew aspirants for healing right up to Reformation times.

Relics, charms, amulets and shrines show the attitude to healing which the Church partly created and partly had to meet. Christianity in many respects was only a thin veneer on the surface of society. Beneath it much of the old paganism lingered on, showing itself particularly, if Dr Margaret Murray is to be believed, in the aberrations of witchcraft. How much there was of real 'spiritual' or 'divine healing' is a matter for speculation. But particularly in the circle of the mystics there must have been a devout spirituality which led to the curing of the whole man. Such healings lie more in the line of modern scientific psychiatry than the matters with which we have hitherto been dealing. Hildegard of Bingen, for instance, once put some nuns who were nervously ill in a butt of cold water full of ants! Formic acid is still used for neurasthenia! There are stories of healings through Luther's prayers, and in certain heretic sects such as the Cathars and the Anabaptists, faith-healing of a more reputable kind brought large renown. Certainly the mystics were long lived. The deeper and more radiant life which came to them through their complete surrender to God enabled them to win the victory over often constant physical disabilities.

After the Reformation the most outstanding example of non-medical healing in the seventeenth century was the king's touch for scrofula; the laying on of hands by a crowned monarch was thought to possess extraordinary healing powers. The position of the king, according to the thought of the time, was not man-made or merely political. He was Gods' anointed, invested by God with powers somewhat analogous to those of bishops. At his coronation he was anointed with the same holy oil as was used in the consecration of priests. In the twelfth and thirteenth centuries the kings of France and England claimed to have the gift of healing, and this, it was said, was in all cases a hereditary gift. Miracles of healing were supposed to have been performed by Robert the Pious in France and Edward the Confessor in England. Elizabeth I exercised the right to touch sufferers from scrofula, a tubercular affection of the skin which might very well yield to the strong power of suggestion made under such circumstances. Tooker, her chaplain, has described for us the deep feeling she had about it and how she prayed to be able to give healing in her hands. Both Charles I and Charles II touched many, not always the poor and ignorant. W. Greenhill wrote to Lady Bacon on 31st December 1629: 'My Lord Anglesey had a daughter cured of the King's Evil with three others on Tuesday.'[8] It is said that Charles II laid hands on no fewer than a hundred thousand persons. It was not only the actual person of the king that was believed to possess this power; a girl from Crewkerne named Elizabeth Parcet is said to

[8] Quoted in Pepys' *Diary* (1904), p. 182, note.

have been cured of scrofula by the Duke of Monmouth when he visited the West Country in the late summer of 1680. Even as late as Queen Anne sovereigns were thought to possess this power, and Boswell tells us how Queen Anne touched the little Samuel Johnson in 1712.[9] After Queen Anne, however, the practice gradually died away, lingering on in the service for anointing drawn up by the Nonjurors and in the usages of the Scottish Episcopal Church. It is curious that though Protestants rejected the healing power of the saints, they kept in increased intensity their faith in the ability of by no means saintly kings to heal them.

Readers of George Fox's *Journal* will remember the accounts of healing that occurred from time to time during his extraordinary ministry. There were many instances among the early Quakers of what today we should call E.S.P., but they kept quiet about such strange happenings, perhaps because they were afraid of being accused of dabbling in 'Papistry'.

What today is known as radiaesthesia seems to have been anticipated in the reign of Charles I. Sir Kenelm Digby invented what he called 'A sympathetic powder' and showed its properties to an assembly of doctors at Montpélier. He claimed that if a bloodstained garment from a wounded person were dipped in water that held in solution some of his powder, it would heal him even if he were far away. Here we have 'absent healing' at work long before the practice of modern times. A colourful figure in the history of faith-healing at this time was Valentine Greatrakes, known as 'the stroker'. He served in the Cromwellian army in Ireland, and in 1662 began to cure not only scrofula but other diseases as well, by the laying on of hands. He performed many cures gratuitously, as we may learn from the 'Brief Account' he wrote of himself in answer to attacks made upon him. Joseph Glanvill describes the gossip at the coffee houses about him, and the marvellous cures he was supposed to have wrought.

Passing into the eighteenth century the outstanding figure in this field is that of Mesmer, with his belief in magnetism and its curative powers. He believed, as Paracelsus had done before him, that there was a mutual interaction between the planets, the earth and living things. This, he thought, was due to an invisible current which he called 'Magnetism'. It was a Jesuit Father, Maximilian Hell, who really set him on his way, for in 1766 Mesmer discovered that the latter was successfully treating disease by stroking

[9] *Life of Johnson* (Birkbeck Hill; 1887), I.42.

the skin with a magnet. Later, in Switzerland, he came across another priest, Father S. S. Gassner, who like the kings, was healing by touch alone. Anticipating what today is known as 'odic force' or radiaesthetic energy, he concluded that certain people were charged with an energy or influence that he called animal magnetism. Soon in Paris people were flocking to the 'magnetic séances' he held round the tub from which projected a series of magnetized iron rods. Finally, since there was so much dispute about the value of his claims, he asked Louis XVI to appoint a commission to investigate his work. This was done in 1784. The report discredited him, since the doctors and scientists composing it declared that the results obtained were purely due to the patient's imagination, and that no such fluid as animal magnetism ever existed. Here we are obviously in the realm of suggestive therapy, later to be taken up by Coué and his 'Nancy School'. Mesmer has a right to be considered one of the pioneers of modern psychotherapy and has a place in the history of faith healing.[10]

The convulsionnaires of St Médard, the miracles of healing which in the 1730's in France were said to have occurred at the tomb of a Jansenist deacon Paris, deserve mention, and according to competent observers at the time were either due to fraud or susceptible of a purely psychological explanation. Apart from these there is not much evidence of directly religious healing being supposed to have taken place. There are very few examples of it in John Wesley's *Journal*. The Methodist revival was concerned with deeper and more important matters. It is true to say that by now what had begun as an integral part of the Church's message to the world had been largely lost. The stream of divine healing has gone underground and will not emerge to the surface again till far on in the nineteenth century. What non-medical healing did persist was divorced from Christian faith and lay more within the province of psychology than of religion.

The belief that disease and suffering were either sent by God or due to sin is still to be found in evangelical circles in the early nineteenth century. John Howard's biographer Field expressed admiration at the wisdom of Providence in killing off Howard's mother, since he might have been spoiled by her. When two of the bishops who censured Tract 90 died, Newman and Pusey thought God had worked a special miracle for their benefit. Edmond Gosse

[10] See also pages 34–6.

tells in *Father and Son* how when he was ill, his father would question him closely as to whether he had committed any sin which could have caused it. When the senior Gosse's book *Omphalos* was met by the critics with a hostile reception, he searched for the sin which could have caused such a calamity. Only gradually did such a caricature of God die away. It led people like John Bright to resist all public health measures and has undoubtedly through the years been responsible for much evil.

Yet that is not the whole story of the early nineteenth century. In Switzerland Dorothea Trudel healed by prayer and anointing, and in spite of official opposition was allowed to go on with her work, since her cures could not be gainsaid. And in America G. O. Barnes, who used the same methods, went about conducting healing missions.

Whatever magical or superstitious practices may have attached themselves to us through the years we have covered in this short sketch, at least the Church's practice of Christian healing has preserved Jesus' thought of God as the compassionate Father of men who seeks their good and not their suffering or misfortune. In that, in spite of all its aberrations and dangers, it has rendered a service not only to medicine, but to the complete welfare of men.

3
Present-day Non-Medical Methods of Healing

Leslie Weatherhead

PRESENT-DAY NON-MEDICAL METHODS OF HEALING

INTRODUCTION

MY TITLE does not in the least suggest a criticism of medical and surgical techniques in the art of healing the sick. These are proved, for all but the hopelessly biased, to have been, and still to be, of immense value to mankind. It is to be remembered that the training of the modern doctor includes every healing method of major importance that has been found valuable since the days of Hippocrates, who flourished in the fifth century before Christ. So highly do I rate these techniques that I feel certain that no progress in the healing art is likely to be made which dissociates itself from them, indeed which does not gladly welcome the contribution to the health of sick people which they have already made, and continue to make.

When this is fully realized, however, it must in all fairness be conceded that the art of healing does not lie only within the province of orthodox medicine.

For example, the healing miracles of Christ would have to be set aside as an irresponsible list of improbable stories unless, sometimes instantaneously, sick people were made well by a word or a touch of Christ. Those who sometimes tell us that the field of healing is the province of the doctor alone ought to recognize that it makes nonsense of the whole ministry of Jesus as recorded in the gospels to say that religion and healing never have anything to do with one another.

I can remember the time when psychology was 'nothing to do with medicine'. This new science was treated with the greatest suspicion. Coué, an early pioneer in introducing some values of suggestion and realizing that they had a bearing on certain cases of illness, was regarded by orthodox medicine as a fool engaged on a 'stunt'. Why, he was not even medically qualified! In the curriculum of the medical student when I was a teenager there were no lectures on psychology. The doctors of fifty years ago said: 'Psychology is nothing to do with us.' Now some of the less enlightened turn to the ministers and say: 'It is nothing to do with you.' They resent ministers being even interested in healing, although Jesus said 'Heal the sick' apparently in the same breath as 'Preach the word', and it is incredible that by the former injunction He meant 'Become a doctor first'.

Surely then, there is a field for what is loosely called 'spiritual healing'. I do not like this term because it seems to imply a slur on other kinds of healing. All healing is of God. No man has ever healed another. All he has done is to co-operate with God either on the physical, psychological, psychical or spiritual level of man's personality. Indeed it seems to me that the first question to be asked by a Christian in the attempt to make any sick person well is: 'Which is the relevant way of co-operating with God in the case of this patient?' It may be surgery or medicine or massage or diet or psychiatry or radiaesthesia or faith or prayer. None is a cure-all. All are of God.

Religion may come into its own in this matter when the doctors really realize that nearly half the patients who take up their time and occupy hospital beds have illnesses which derive from one fact: namely, that in the deep mind of the patient an unhealthy emotion, one inimical to the well-being of the whole man, is imprisoned. Repressed and therefore unconscious, resentment, hate, worry, exaggerated and irrational fear, envy, malice and uncharitableness, and above all guilt, poison not only the mind but the body. Sanity is not so often threatened, but the emotional life of the patient is disturbed and gets itself translated into physical illness. The emotional part of the mind has a way of handing over its dis-ease to the body and at some weak link, some constitutional defect, or, in certain cases, in some charade-like[1] illness which mimes the emotional cause, we have a patient who can be *eased* by drugs, tonics, injections, rest and a cruise in the Mediterranean, but only *cured* when his emotional malaise is unearthed and dispelled.

Ministers, who frankly are frequently despised by some doctors who patronize them and think that any fool could do their kind of job, have immense power in their hands. In their pastoral visiting they could—with very little more training—spot quickly amongst the children of the families in their care, the early development of those neuroses which can make a patient break down in his forties.

---

[1] E.g. the patient who developed a 'tic' or compulsive twitch of the head and neck which began as he tried to dodge falling timber in an air raid.

Ministers with more training could, without treading on the toes of the medical profession, offer to have what I call therapeutic conversations with various patients, aimed at getting—say—the hate or resentment against man and God out of their deep minds. And ministers in their pulpit work could, and often do, so preach, that men would, during a single hour's service, exchange hate for love, guilt for forgiveness, worry for trust, fear for courage, malice for kindness, and thus be saved countless ills. When all is revealed, many ministers who suffer from inferiority will stand delighted and amazed to learn of the grand job they did merely in the field of preventive medicine by the faithful proclamation of the Gospel.

In this paper I shall try to deal with non-medical methods of healing, whether by what is called 'spiritual healing' or not. Surgery done by a real Christian—as it is done by a friend of mine who always prays before he operates—is also spiritual healing, but let us look together at some of the methods which are normally outside the province of the general practitioner of medicine.

I divide these methods as follows—

(1) Methods which involve Suggestion:
    Auto-Suggestion, Mesmerism, and Hypnotism
    Christian Science and Lourdes
(2) Methods which involve Psychic Research:
    Spiritualism and 'Spirit Healers'
    Odic Force
(3) The Minister and Public Methods:
    Healing Missions
    The Public 'Laying on of Hands'
    Intercession for the Sick
(4) The Minister and Private Methods:
    The Place of Confession
    Psychotherapeutic Conversations
    The Minister and his attitude to Psychiatric treatment

I

METHODS WHICH INVOLVE SUGGESTION

Auto-Suggestion

THESE methods go back, of course, as far as human history, and are still in daily use. 'Mummy kiss it better' or its ancient equivalent has been an age-long way of treating childhood's ills of body, and 'the power of positive thinking' is enshrined in every religion in the world.

Emile Coué who died in 1926 made world-popular his method of auto-suggestion. Patients, whatever their ills, were to repeat with uncritical minds the magic slogan: 'Every day in every way I am getting better and better.' The will was not to be engaged. It was the imagination that had the greater power. There must be no negatives in the affirmation, no future tenses, no diagnosis of the trouble. So a hundred people a day thronged Coué's garden and the movement swept the civilized world.

There is no doubt that we have here a method of immense value in certain cases. Indeed, a great deal of preaching is really therapeutic, because, while it calls for faith, it is effective through the mechanisms of suggestion. 'I can do all things through Christ who strengtheneth me' seems to me an invaluable piece of auto-suggestion.

Where the method would be dangerous would be in a case of undiagnosed illness. In such a case auto-suggestion might postpone a more relevant treatment until the latter was too late. Another danger is the removal by suggestion of a symptom which to a doctor would be a signpost leading him to diagnose the true cause and nature of the illness.

Again, the method will not work with unsuggestible people and suggestibility must be differentiated from faith. Faith has to be fought for, but it can be the possession of all. Suggestibility is a characteristic which one either has or has not, though it can be increased or decreased. Its causes are obscure. They are not related to education, and to be suggestible, though useful, has its drawbacks, and is neither to the credit nor discredit of its possessor.

If, however, the mind can be persuaded to accept a reasonable idea, then the idea tends to actualize or come true, and in many cases this principle opens up a valuable method of helping *some* sick folk.

Mesmerism

Mesmer (1733–1815) need not keep us long in this brief survey of non-medical ways of healing. He wrote about what he called 'animal magnetism'. He actually used magnets but more significantly passes with his hands, still referred to as 'mesmerism'. He was rather a showman.

We are to imagine a large, luxurious salon hung with mirrors, furnished with beautiful curtains, filled with exotic flowers, illumined by stained-glass windows, perfumed with incense burning in beautiful antique bowls. 'Aeolian harps sighed melodious music from distant chambers, while sometimes a sweet, female voice, from above or below, stole softly upon the mysterious silence.' In the centre of a room there was a circular oak tub, the bottom filled with powdered glass and iron filings. On this lay bottles immersed in water, some with necks to the centre of the tub and others pointing to its circumference. Covering the tub was a lid pierced by many holes through which had been passed iron rods, bent so as to be able to be grasped by patients grouped about the tub. In absolute silence the patients sat in several rows. They held one another's hands if the latter were not engaged by holding one of the iron rods. If a rod could be applied to the ailing spot, so much the better.

Then, with appropriate music, Mesmer appeared in a lilac robe of finest silk. In his hand was a long, iron wand, powerfully magnetized. He passed slowly among the patients, fixing them with his staring eyes, making passes with his hands and touching them with his wand. Many, we are told, recovered. Many passed into convulsive states or delirium, and these symptoms were welcomed and called 'the crisis'.

But instead of scientific research which might have led somewhere, Mesmer propounded a cast-iron theory and tried to push all the facts into it—the opposite of the scientific method. He magnetized water and sold it to patients. He magnetized their clothes. They ate from magnetized plates and breathed a magnetized atmosphere. A patient had only to carry some magnetized charm and he could not fall ill. In a word, Mesmer, instead of taking the forward path of science, took a retrogressive path back towards magic, incantation and spell. Money flowed in, and his name was honoured for a time, but when challenged by scientific authority he prepared a paper full of false assumptions and unproved claims.[2]

These claims were rejected by special commissions of inquiry, but the fact remains that some patients recovered, and their recovery points to the value of suggestion in some cases.

Mesmer's work prepared the way for hypnotism, and here we

[2] I have quoted here from my book, *Psychology, Religion and Healing* (Hodder & Stoughton), in which all these methods are dealt with at greater length.

must linger a little longer, for, in my opinion, hypnosis still has great value both in getting ideas of a therapeutic and reassuring nature *into* a patient's mind and also in releasing from the deep mind those 'forgotten' events which, because a buried unhealthy emotion still clings to them, and because conflict is still set up by them, can prevent a patient from attaining that mental integrity and unity on which health depends.

Hypnotism

It is still difficult to say what hypnotism actually is. We know that it is 'a kind of sleep' as the word suggests. But the patient is *en rapport* with the hypnotist throughout, and, unless differently instructed, is 'asleep' to everyone else and quite unresponsive. Hypnosis has been described as a state of increased suggestibility, but such language rather tells us the characteristics of a state of mind than explains what the state of mind is. Hypnosis has been described as 'a state of mental dissociation', but the same comment holds. There is much that is obscure. We know that the fear of being hypnotized—a fear which may be based on ignorance, or impossible film stories, or fictitious scenes in novels, or the witnessing of the deplorable tricks of a stage hypnotist—can make a person unhypnotizable; but even without such fear, only a small proportion of patients, in my experience of forty years, go into really deep hypnosis, though most people can, with patience, be made hypnoidal. They become sleepy and more suggestible than they normally are.

Hypnosis is not being more and more widely used for several reasons. One is that it is not completely understood. Another is that it has had a rather questionable history and thus is regarded in some quarters with suspicion. Another is that its results are sometimes disappointingly short-lived. The hypnotist may fall to the temptation to remove the symptom without dealing with its cause; this could be a highly dangerous procedure. Another is that the modern discoveries of drugs mean that the medically qualified practitioner has a short cut by means of injections which give him a more certain and dependable result without many of the disadvantages just listed.

No one, however, should view the induction of hypnosis as *dangerous* to a patient. I have hypnotized hundreds of people without one harmful result. If one hypnotizes the same patient some hundreds of times, I suspect that one makes him emotionally

dependent on one, but that is a matter that can be dealt with.
It has been supposed that a person who is deeply hypnotized lays himself or herself open to sexual assault or that he could be made to carry out a criminal act. The truth is that unless the subject is already sexually depraved or a criminal, the hypnotic suggestion would be rejected. The literature here makes it clear that the subject would probably wake up.[3]

At the same time, Janet notes five cases of rape which took place under hypnosis. If the patient really trusted the hypnotist, the latter might do an unworthy thing without the patient waking up. It is also to be remembered that the patient may *imagine* that he has been assaulted or robbed, so that unless the patient is well known to the hypnotist and trusted by him, it is well to have a witness present.

Another important point to remember is that it is insufficient to get the patient only to recall during hypnosis the buried traumatic incidents that set up his present distress. The hypnotic session must include the suggestion that on awakening, the patient will consciously recall and re-tell the incidents and that he will *feel* again the emotion he felt then.

A suggestion has been made that only the medically qualified should be legally allowed to induce hypnosis. As one who has taught many doctors how to hypnotize a patient, I am strongly against this. The minister of the future should surely be included in any list of those qualified to induce hypnosis. He can easily be taught all that is known about it, how to induce it and what is to be expected from it. I rather suspect, and certainly believe, a tendency to make the medical profession a kind of closed shop, vesting in doctors power which should be shared. Ministers are as capable of learning as doctors. They are not fools, nor are they more likely to abuse power or—in the matter under discussion—more likely to make a sexual assault on a hypnotized person. Remembering the great shortage of doctors equipped in this field, and the immense spiritual value of hypnotic suggestion and of what could be called hypno-confession, it seems clear that ministers should not be forbidden to induce hypnosis. Any minister adequately trained—say by taking our Methodist

---

[3] See my *Psychology, Religion and Healing* (Hodder & Stoughton, 5th edn., pp. 124 ff), and my *Psychology in Service of the Soul* (Epworth, 20th edn., p. 134). See also Janet, *Psychological Healing*, I.184ff, and Maudsley, *Pathology of Mind*, p. 52.

post graduate diploma in pastoral psychology—should feel equipped, and is better equipped than the average G.P., to enter this field and use this method.

Christian Science

I shall not deal with Christian Science at great length, because I have already done this in my book *Psychology, Religion and Healing*,[4] where forty pages are devoted to considering the person of Mrs Eddy, her fantastic book called *Science and Health*, and the false theories underlying the practice.

It is true that some important truths lie behind Christian Science and that many of its adherents are sincere and loving people. Its scope and widespread influence are a challenge to the modern Christian Church which should teach all that is true in Christian Science and practise all that is of value.

For some people it is of immense value that they should not dwell on their pain or adopt negative attitudes to it. There *is* a reality about the spiritual part of the universe unshared by the material. Health often *is* attained when unity with God is increased. It turns out again and again that the illness from which many a patient suffered was fundamentally a dis-ease of mind or spirit. To get men to realize this and to win them to an attitude which ignores self and seeks unity with God is a great and good thing to do.

But of course we do not need the teachings of the neurotic and uneducated Mrs Eddy to achieve this. Her book, often quite unintelligible nonsense borrowed, it is said, from the writings of a 'magnetizer' called Quimby and reduced to English by a paid hack called Henry Wiggin, is a fantastic maze of bewildering and often meaningless sentences.

Her treatments have had their successes because mental suggestion and a resolute turning of the mind to God and ideas of His perfection are in some neurotically caused illnesses just the treatment that is needed, but, if Christian Science were universally adopted, the security we have laboured for in combating disease would disappear. We should be back amid the devastating killing epidemics which decimated the population in the old days of superstition and ignorance.

Consider this sentence from *Science and Health* (p. 389): 'The less we know or think about hygiene, the less we are predisposed

[4] See pp. 160–200.

to sickness.' In India I remember a village in which cholera broke out. It was found that discharges from the bodies of cholera patients seeped into the common well from which the whole village took its drinking-water. Real science, finding this, took steps which checked the epidemic. Ignorance of hygiene, continuing, would have decimated the whole community. Is the word 'nonsense' too strong? Is it not clear that Christian Scientists could not live in a society which practised their own beliefs? They are parasitic on a community that has developed a security which their teachings would destroy. They exist through precautions based on a philosophy which contradicts their own. As Fisher says: 'A strict execution of Mrs Eddy's doctrines throughout the world would, in a very few years, extinguish human life upon this planet.'[5]

Consider Mrs. Eddy's treatment of a boil. 'You say a boil is painful, but that is impossible, for matter without mind is not painful. The boil simply manifests, through inflammation and swelling, a belief in pain and this belief is called a boil. Now administer mentally to your patient *a high attenuation of truth* and it will soon cure the boil.'[6]

I am afraid that the character of Mrs Eddy, whom the famous lawyer Peabody called 'the champion fraud and impostor of the age', the character of her book, and the danger of Christian Science practice, refusing as it so often does to discriminate between one kind of disease and another, and turned with unconscious cruelty on to suffering little children, must compel any thoughtful person to dismiss Christian Science as a dangerous superstition and answer its challenge in a way more faithful to Christ and the integrity of the human mind to which He paid so great a respect.

Lourdes

In 1858 on the Thursday before Lent a young girl of fourteen years of age, who like so many at that age was very religiously suggestible, had a number of visions of the Virgin Mary at Lourdes in the South of France. On the first occasion of these visions the child was with a sister and a friend, but they saw and heard nothing. Bernadette alleged that the Virgin directed her to scratch at the earth in an indicated spot, whereupon water gushed forth which has flowed ever since. The Virgin also gave instructions

[5] H. A. L. Fisher on 'Our New Religion' (Ernest Benn; 1929), p. 163.
[6] *Science and Health*, p. 153.

that a church was to be built there, healing processions arranged, and facilities made for bathing in the stream.

This has been faithfully carried out. When I visited Lourdes in 1949, ten thousand other pilgrims did the same, though in that pilgrimage not one of the hundreds of sick people who visited Lourdes even claimed a cure. Indeed, Dr George Day in the Hunterian Oration of 1952, wrote as follows: 'The complete cure of bodily ailments has only happened to 200 patients out of 68 million who have been reported on—a matter of ·0003 per cent. The real miracle of Lourdes is the change of personality of the many who make the pilgrimage. They come back with a changed attitude towards their illness or incapacity—an attitude of active acceptance—with an eagerness to help others achieve the same happiness. They have triumphed over their disease. I have a strong suspicion that this miracle begins the moment the patient decides to set out. A patient sets out to see his doctor in hope but driven by fear. A pilgrimage is an Act of Faith with Hope but with no compulsion of Fear.'

I will not attempt to deal exhaustively with the problems set up by Lourdes, because I have done this already.[7] In my opinion Bernadette had a hallucination.[8] This is no disparagement. Hallucination is not an uncommon experience. Further, we must remember the religious feelings of a young girl at puberty and the fact that the garments in which the Virgin appeared were similar to those worn by members of a girls' guild to which Bernadette belonged.

Bernadette, dressed in such clothes, had recently taken part in the funeral of the Guild's President, Mademoiselle Latapie, who had mothered all the girls in the Guild. When Bernadette described her visions to a friend, the latter identified the lady, not as the Virgin, but as Mademoiselle Latapie. The words spoken, 'I am the Immaculate Conception', are to us meaningless. But we know that in 1854, four years before the vision, the Pope had declared that dogma an Article of the Faith of all Roman Catholics, and that Bernadette's priest, Monsieur Peyramale, had preached on it just previous to Bernadette's vision. Thus we can to some extent understand the 'build up' of the hallucination.

Valuable as a visit to Lourdes no doubt is to the Roman Catholic

---

[7] See *Psychology, Religion and Healing*, pp. 147ff.
[8] The differences between a hallucination and an apparition I have set out in *The Resurrection of Christ* (Epworth Press), pp. 66ff.

pilgrim from the point of view of a religious experience, its value as a therapeutic agency can be ignored. Indeed, one correspondent wrote to me alleging that a specimen of the healing waters of Lourdes taken from the baths into which the sacred stream runs was found on laboratory examination to contain typhoid bacilli. Having seen the condition of the water in these baths I can well believe it, though as yet no epidemic of disease has been traced to Lourdes. When this water has been analysed, however, scientists have been unanimous in stating that it has contained no ingredients of any therapeutic value.

Bernadette herself was a life-long sufferer from asthma and died of this disease. The inhabitants of Lourdes and the neighbourhood show no evidence of having at the door a remedy for human ailments. Some among the few cured do not believe in any form of Christianity. Some are atheists whose mental attitude is 'Try anything once; it cannot do harm'. Some are cured before they reach Lourdes, some after they return home.

As a healing agency Lourdes is negligible.

2

METHODS WHICH INVOLVE PSYCHIC RESEARCH

WHAT are we to make of healers like Mr Harry Edwards, who believes that he is controlled by the spirits of Lister and Pasteur, long since dead, and that they take possession of him, guide him to the seat of a patient's troubles and work through the hands he lays upon them? Many healers seem to have similar power in their fingers, and naturally, as one keenly interested in this subject, I have studied them and their methods carefully. Mr Harry Edwards came to my home and laid hands on ten selected patients whom I myself had quite failed to benefit by psychological-cum-spiritual treatment. He failed also.

When I went with the late Dr Sangster to Mr Edwards's centre in Shere, near Guildford, watched him at work and discussed matters with him, I came to some very definite conclusions. The first and most important was a belief in his complete sincerity. There is nothing of the quack or showman about him. He was, I believe, a printer's compositor who discovered that he had this strange power of healing some people and who determined to let suffering mankind benefit by it. All honour and credit to him. I have no evidence that he is motivated by any desire to make money or to attain fame. I am not myself convinced that his philosophy of life is sound and I am sceptical about the idea that Lister and Pasteur have anything to do with his successes, but I will deal with that later.

The second conclusion I came to was that he does have remarkable and genuine successes. I am aware of the report on his work published after the researches into it carried out by Dr Louis Rose. I heard Dr Rose make his report. But I am also aware of the extreme scepticism of some members of the medical profession and their reluctance to admit that sometimes sick people get well without any reference to them. On at least one occasion on television Mr Edwards had in my opinion a raw deal. Phrases like 'faulty diagnosis' and 'expected recession' can be glibly used, and the claim that, Edwards or no Edwards, the patient would in any case have got well can easily be made when, had an orthodox medical method been used, the resulting cure would have been attributed to its efficacy.

What then is this strange gift which *in certain cases* does bring about relief and sometimes permanent cure? I believe it to be a 'gift' about which little is known, but which may have been the gift of healing about which St Paul speaks (1 Cor 12^{28}), a gift which is very ancient and which has nothing essentially to do with religion. It does seem to be hereditary, though in my opinion it is possessed by a great many more people than are aware of it and *may* be to some extent possessed by all. It has been called radiaesthetic energy or, the term I prefer, odic force.

Lest it should be thought that I am romancing, I hasten to add that I have addressed in London a meeting of doctors called 'The Medical Society for the Study of Radiaesthesia'. They have their headquarters near Harley Street, issue reports from time to time, and have regular lectures delivered which I have had the privilege of attending. Some of these doctors use this odic force in their treatments. One, in Harley Street, has become a close friend of mine, and, though his theories need further exposition and clarification, I have seen some of his amazing results with my own eyes and can give a personal testimony to their value.

The term 'odic force' is the one which I prefer and shall use here. It derives from Odin, or Odan, or Wotan, the god of ancient Norse mythology, who was the Scandinavian counterpart of Jupiter or Zeus, and whose power permeated everything in heaven and earth. One might call 'odic force' the all-pervading energy. It was discovered or rediscovered a hundred years ago, though its discoverer was scorned, derided, insulted, and then ignored. Now, in my opinion, inquiry into it is leading us into a conception of a part of the universe as epoch-making and wonderful as astronomy has made the starry heavens and as nuclear physics has made atomic energy.

In Stuttgart from 1788 to 1869 lived a brilliant chemist called Karl von Reichenbach. His ability as a chemist was recognized by all. He was not a doctor of medicine, but a Ph.D., and the discoverer of both creosote and paraffin (1830).

His researches into magnetism led him to a discovery which perhaps he would never have made had he not had the help of what is technically called a 'sensitive'—i.e. a person with abnormal psychic powers, including clairvoyance. Reichenbach found that 'sensitives' could see apparent emanations from a magnetized bar which they described as streams of light. Reichenbach himself was not a 'sensitive', but he discovered that 'sensitives' could also see such emanations from certain metals, crystals, from matter which was undergoing chemical change, and *from the human body*, much more marked with some people, but discernible in all.

Reichenbach first thought that this power was a quality of magnetism. He tried many experiments with it, and it was he who called it 'odic force' because he believed it penetrated everything. He also thought it to be similar to light, and in 1850 he published a four-volume work called *The Laws of Odic Light*. But later he declared that, though it was a real force which could be measured (e.g. he estimated that it took thirty seconds to traverse one hundred feet of iron wire of a stated calibre), it differed from heat, electricity, magnetism, or light.

Reichenbach in his ponderous treatise[9] described many things which stretch the credulity of one who comes newly to the subject. He found, for instance, that the hand of a 'sensitive' adhered to a magnet 'as a piece of iron does', and that water which had been in contact with a strong magnet could be distinguished by a 'sensitive' from ordinary water. A strong magnet caused the hand and arm of a cataleptic medium to move towards it as far as the body would

---

[9] *Researches on Magnetism, Electricity, Heat, Light, Crystallization and Chemical Attraction in their relations to the Vital Force*, by Karl Baron von Reichenbach, Ph.D., translated by William Gregory, M.D., F.R.S.E., Professor of Chemistry in the University of Edinburgh (Taylor, Watson & Maberley, London 1850).

allow.[10] He found, moreover, that water could be 'odicized', by using the fingers of the hand, which, to the sensitive, produced the same results as a magnet. To grasp a sensitive, as we do when shaking hands, produced a disagreeable feeling, but to grasp both hands, right to left and left to right, produced a warm and comfortable sensation. Reichenbach writes: 'When I gave my hands to Mr Incledon and above all when I crossed them, he felt an intolerable headache.'[11]

Reichenbach holds that this power resides potently in the sun,[12] but permeates the earth and everything upon it. All things conduct it, but loosely woven materials (like a net) hamper its flow, and silk partly insulates it. We now know that nylon completely blocks it. Iron wire carries it successfully, and odic force was detected by a sensitive after it had passed along an iron wire 33 feet long and 0·0794 of an inch thick. The force was seen by the sensitive as 'a slender column of flame, 10 to $13\frac{1}{2}$ inches long with a breadth of 0·8 of an inch'.[13]

Odic force appears to increase in a person after taking food, being in the sunshine, and by general physical fitness. Reichenbach writes: 'Trials with Mademoiselle Maix and M. Schuh yielded the same results [as those he had reached earlier]. They both found my hands more powerful after dinner than before it.'[14] The light diffused by bodies possessing this force is exceedingly feeble and is not visible to every eye. Psychic sensitives see it. Other people, not psychically very sensitive, see it if they remain two hours in complete darkness. Then their eyes are frequently sufficiently prepared to perceive this light. During the two hours the eye must not be reached by the smallest trace of any other light.[15] Even a sensitive, he adds, 'cannot with certainty perceive magnetic light at a greater distance than 40 inches'.[16] Odic force resides in magnets, crystals, the hands, the sun, the moon, in artificial light,

---

[10] Ibid. p. 25.
[11] Ibid. pp. 81–2 and 177.
[12] Ibid. p. 96. Reichenbach believes that the magnetism of the earth acts as a magnet in the laboratory and discharges odic force. He taught that if people would arrange their beds with the head to the north and the feet to the south, they would sleep better, because the lines of force would run with, and not against, the lines of force in the body.
[13] Ibid. pp. 100–2.
[14] Ibid. p. 196.
[15] Ibid. p. 214.
[16] Ibid. p. 355.

and in any matter undergoing chemical change, such as an acid or an alkali or an organic body undergoing decomposition.

Research into odic force is in its infancy. Very little is known, and I have a hunch that in the field of psychic research and by investigation into the so-called aura that surrounds the human body, we may find clues which will help us to understand. Perhaps, indeed, psychic research will make us alter altogether the very primitive and elementary ideas we have about this form of energy. It is alleged by some writers that healing odic force can be most readily introduced into the body at the chakrams, as they are called, that is, the 'power centres' of the etheric body which covers and to a short distance overlaps the physical body.

It is said that one's right hand is negative and one's left positive; and that a psychically sensitive person—unless left-handed—would prefer to have his left hand shaken rather than his right, for then negative flows to positive and is not repelled by its like. It is alleged that a sensitive can tell in which hand a person possessing odic force has held a glass of drinking-water. Held in the right hand (the negative one) the water tastes pleasant; held in the left (the positive) it has an unpleasant taste. Conversely, if a glass of water is placed in the blue light of the spectrum, the water to a sensitive will thereafter taste cool, pleasant, and slightly acid. A glass of water in orange or yellow light will subsequently taste to a sensitive nauseating, bitter, and distasteful.

A definition of odic force is difficult. I can only offer that put forward by Reichenbach himself in one of his letters. He defines it as 'a current of energy which emanates from certain organic and inorganic bodies, including human bodies, plants, magnets, crystals, and so on'. He thought it was conducted through all bodies which are continuous in structure. He thought that it accounted for the phenomenon of table-turning and the 'passes' made by the hands of the old-fashioned mesmerist.

He believed also that the curious behaviour of a pendulum, let us say of a pellet of cork hung on a thin silken thread, was determined by odic force. If the right hand of a sensitive touches the point from which a pendulum is suspended, the latter will swing. In his letters, Reichenbach refers to an experiment which he says proves that the right hand of a sensitive glows in the dark with a blue flame, the left with a yellowish-red flame. It is alleged that putrefaction gives off odic light, and the queer phosphorescence which sensitives have claimed to see over some of the graves in cemeteries may find explanation here. When a long period has elapsed after death, no phosphorescent light is seen even by sensitives, for putrefaction has ceased.

Odic force, Reichenbach tells us, is discharged through the fingers and to some extent through the breath.[17] It is faster than heat in travelling and slower than electricity. It is not, like the latter, conducted over the surface of a conductor, but permeates it wholly. It is retained for some time in matter charged by it, and it is retained longest in oil. It is interesting that oil 'blessed' by being held in a bishop's *hand* was used in the healing services of the early Church.

Science up to now has rejected the theory of odic force largely because science has not invented an instrument with which to measure it. It does not affect the thermometer, or any other instrument in general use. Yet now scientists are considering it again, and it may well be that at our very finger-tips we have an energy of unpredictable value.

I recently watched some interesting experiments on a purely scientific basis, and without reference to religion, by a medically qualified friend in the neighbourhood of Harley Street, whom I will call Dr X and who has read and approved this essay. He has in a marked degree this power, which Mrs Salmon has and which I think Mr Harry Edwards, Brother Mandus and others have. It is capable of producing muscular movements or twitchings in some patients. Whatever it is, it is frequently felt as heat. Some time ago Dr X held his extended hands a few inches from the skin of my bare shoulders—I had had some fibrositis—and all day my shoulders burned as if they had been poulticed. The pain disappeared. A friend of mine, a bishop, had his fibrositis banished in a few moments by Dr X in the same way. Mrs Salmon's hands, she tells us, communicate this kind of heat.

But the mystery deepens. It is well known that psychically sensitive people, called 'dowsers' or 'water diviners', can detect the unseen presence of water because their muscles twitch when they pass over it. They frequently hold in their hands a twig, but it is their muscles, not the twigs, which are sensitive. The theory is that every substance sends out waves of a psychic kind, and the wave-length differs according to the substance that transmits it. The emanation of energy from the diviner meets the emanation from the water, and their meeting sets up a muscle spasm. These

[17] Cf. Elijah healing the widow's son (1 Kings 17[17]).

wave-lengths can be measured. Dr X showed me his chart with the calculated wave-length set up by every element known to chemistry. He recently 'discovered' a precious metal under a lonely moor by this method. His ideas were vindicated when engineers acted on his instructions and brought the metal to the surface.

Now conditions of disease, it is alleged, throw out varying wave-lengths according to the nature of the illness. The tubercle bacillus, for instance, or TB germs, send out wave-lengths which have been measured and which a psychically sensitive person can 'feel'. I was shown a bottle of TB germs at one end of a brass ruler divided into inches, and then shown an instrument which at regular distances (representing the wave-length) 'detected' the presence of TB. This instrument placed near the lungs of a TB patient gives the same indication at the same distances, and thus confirms a TB diagnosis.

Where there is pain in the body, psychic energy is being lost, much as static electricity is 'lost' by running to earth. At this 'pain-point', by holding his hands in a certain position almost touching the skin, Dr X appears to drive his own odic force into a body, and to do so powerfully enough to send it up the nerve paths to the seat of the pain, often with what appear to be miraculously therapeutic results. This seems to be what Mrs Salmon does, though she calls it the power of Christ, and what Mr Edwards does, though he believes it to be force passed through him by the power of spirits on the other side of death. Dr X believes it to be a perfectly normal form of energy, not yet understood, but rapidly coming under the survey and understanding of science.

The most remarkable thing I have seen in my visits to Dr X's rooms was the case of a girl with a twisted pelvis, who, when he placed his hands near, but not touching her thighs, twisted her body in a most strange way. He said the body was trying to heal itself, to correct the faulty twist, in response to the force passing from his hands meeting the discharge of psychic energy from her pain, much as a water-diviner's hands twitch in response to the emanations from water. I found to my amazement that I could induce this reaction in her also.

Remarkable to me—who am not consciously sensitive in the psychic sense—was the discovery that, when asked by Dr X to tell him which part of a patient's back was causing her distress, as she lay face downward on his couch with her back exposed, I had only to run my hand down the length of the spinal column, a few inches from the skin surface, to feel unmistakably a sensation of pins and needles in my hand at one particular point, which turned out to be the focus-point of the pain. Dr X said that emanations from the pain-spot met the odic force from my own hand and set up the sensation in the latter.

On another occasion I took the late Bishop of Lichfield, Dr Woods, to see Dr X, and one of the latter's patients was a little girl of three who had been discharged from a famous children's hospital in London, her mother being told that the child had been injured at birth and would never walk. I held my own hands with Dr X in the appropriate place at the base of the spine, and our delight can be imagined when the child moved her legs for the first time in her life, and said: 'Mummy, I can move my legs.' The mother was overcome with tears of joy, and indeed the Bishop and all of us were deeply moved. The child can now get into a crouching position, and with a good deal of help can stand on her feet and walk a few steps.

It may be that here we have a clue to the understanding of the undoubted healing gift which some people possess, and I must say that investigation in the radiaesthetic field seems to me more likely to bear fruit than investigation into spiritualism, where it is supposed that the so-called dead return and possess certain people and guide them to locate injury and treat the sufferer. I am not deriding the spiritualistic hypothesis, however, for there again some truth seems to me concealed amongst error.

The uncanny way in which some spiritualist healers find the correct spot where pain and disability and disease lurk, and do so often without being told by the patient or his friends where the pain is or what the diagnosis may be, is possibly due to the sensation set up in the hand by odic force in the manner described above.

Researchers have been working in this field for many years, but it must be said that only a beginning has been made. The difficulties are enormous, and the prejudice against unorthodoxy in healing methods—while it probably safeguards patients against cranks, charlatans, and fanatics, and prevents treatment running too far ahead of theory and understanding—slows down the rate of progress.

Twenty years ago a specimen of blood from the finger of one

of my children, sent on a bit of blotting paper to a 'radiaesthetist', led her, by holding a pendulum over it and over certain bio-chemic salts, to prescribe a remedy which entirely cured a most obstinate and long-standing disability which had made the child's life miserable for years.

Today if a diagnosis is doubtful, you may send a spot of blood to a laboratory in a famous city and receive not only a confirmation or otherwise of the diagnosis; *you can actually receive a photograph of the affected part* showing the damaged structures. Though the patient may have remained all the time in London, the blood-spot emits radiations which disclose to the scientist working there the exact nature and scope of the disharmony. Each disease radiates its own characteristic wave-form and a method has been found whereby a 'force-field' photograph can be taken of 'the condition of any cell-group in the body', the photograph showing not only the pathology but the state of the tissues involved. I have actually seen a photograph of the tuberculous lungs of a patient, showing clearly the extent of the disease, taken while the patient lay in a London hospital. *The instrument which took the photograph was fifty miles away*. All that was required on the spot was a drop of the patient's blood or a specimen of sputum. I have also seen a 'photograph' of a cow's stomach showing the presence in it of a length of wire and a large stone. *It was taken forty miles from the cow*. A veterinary surgeon confirmed the experiment by removing both wire and stone.

If, by this time, the reader is about to declare that he cannot be asked to believe such nonsense, I will only remind him that fifty years ago, if someone had told him that, by watching a screen in his home, he could see and hear in London something that was happening *at that precise moment* in Edinburgh, let alone New York, he would have made a similar reply. We are moving forward to discover that there are energies at work in the universe more wonderful than we have dared to dream.

I have written at length on odic force because it is so little known, but in this section I do not wish to rule out some possibilities in what is loosely called spiritualism.

When every allowance has been made for deceit, for the false conclusions of the self-deceived, for alternative hypotheses, and for co-incidences, I am myself convinced that occasionally those whom we call the dead do get through to us. Our health may well be their loving concern. I have myself known cases in which life has been saved through intervention from 'the other side'.[18] The phenomena of psychometry shout aloud for investigation. The work of sincere clairvoyants is worthy of scientific investigation.[19] The *Proceedings of the Society for Psychical Research* contain evidences of messages which have come through mediums from doctors 'on the other side' and the messages have led to revised diagnoses, changed treatments, and the saving of life.[20]

Recourse to spiritualism when a dear one is desperately ill is the last field of inquiry I should be willing to explore. At the same time truth comes through strange doors and it would seem to me unscientific and obtuse to decide beforehand that through any particular door no saving truth could possibly emerge. The universe does not end at the point where our five senses cease to register its phenomena, and it may be that truth may break forth from what—for want of better terms—we label the psychic level, confounding our reluctance and our doubts, and bringing to our aid sources of untapped energy and power close at hand and yet undreamed of and but little understood.

3

THE MINISTER AND PUBLIC METHODS

Healing Missions

IF sick people can possibly be made well it is a very serious thing to disparage any method of achieving such a worthwhile end.

Yet, in my opinion, if the uninstructed public is admitted and an indiscriminate invitation is given to people to come forward at a service for the public laying on of hands on the part of a 'healer', then the dangers are so great that the enterprise should not be undertaken. As I shall show later, the laying on of hands in a patient's room or in a small chapel in the presence of a few prayerful friends, after the patient has been carefully instructed, is another matter.

Let us look at the dangers of a much advertised mission which anyone may attend and during which anyone may come forward for healing.

---

[18] I have cited some examples in *Psychology, Religion and Healing*, pp. 214ff.
[19] E.g. the work of Miss Phoebe Payne (Ibid. p. 215) and of Miss Geraldine Cummins.
[20] Vol. IX, pp. 182ff.

In the first place—and most importantly—a certain degree of emotion is inevitable. The advertising of a 'healing service' always draws a crowd. One minister I knew, baffled by an empty downtown church, filled it in a fortnight by advertising healing-services. The suggestibility—not the faith, which is very different—of a hysterical patient is enormously increased by the presence, expectancy, and excitement of the crowd. This atmosphere is often deliberately increased in intensity by the singing of certain hymns. In one which I attended, a sentimental chorus with the phrase 'No never alone', repeated again and again, was sung perhaps a dozen times. It was almost crooned. In Lourdes I heard them singing '*Ave, Ave, Ave Maria*' in the same way until one was sick of both words and tune.

Now the great danger of this emotion to the hysterical type of patient is that his *symptom*, not the cause of it, can frequently be made to disappear. I well remember in Leeds the case of Miss A who was lame. Joyously on a certain Tuesday she declared herself healed by Pastor X in front of a crowd of people in a large hall. She there and then threw away her crutches and walked off the platform without them. This was widely publicized. The next evening her photograph was in the papers and by Thursday she was receiving hundreds of letters from distressed people. Should they make the journey to Leeds to attend the mission? Should they bring their relatives and friends? She appealed to me to know what to do, and while the excitement lasted she walked without aid.

Alas, in less than three weeks Miss A had purchased new crutches and resumed her handicapped life with her mind tortured by some very difficult questions about God and faith and Pastor X, and the value of healing-missions.

But sometimes a worse thing happens. In the excitement and hysterical emotion, one symptom is sometimes *permanently* removed only to be followed by one far more baffling to the patient's doctors. Unless the *cause* of the symptoms is not only disclosed and emotionally realized but also faced in a new and healthier way, the unconscious mind is liable to produce a symptom which has a more tenacious grip of the patient. Indeed, the physical symptom can be replaced by a mental one and the last state of the patient be worse than the first. The saints have always reminded us that it is better to bear our ills in the body than in the mind. Indeed, much psychosomatic illness is set up because a troubled mind has a way of handing over its dis-ease to the body. Sometimes a congenital weakness is seized upon by the unconscious, or perhaps a condition is imposed which gets the patient out of some strain he wants to avoid, or perhaps a condition like headache or rheumatism or even a bad cold is continued and made chronic because it can physically express the emotional dis-ease of the patient.

Indeed, it is sometimes perilous to remove a physical symptom. Some patients have become insane after the *physical* symptom of their mal-adjustment to reality has been removed and could no longer express their mal-adjustment in physical terms. So Jesus was not using a threat, but stating a sheer fact of our mental make-up, when He said to one patient, 'Sin no more, *lest a worse thing befall thee*' (John 5^{14}).

Jesus, it seems to me, had far more in common with a modern surgeon or physician than with a modern faith healer. Both surgeon and physician know what is wrong and direct and alter their technique accordingly. They have the skill and character to *call out* the patient's faith. A modern faith healer frequently does not understand at all what is wrong. He uses the same method for every case, and his many failures are put down to the patients' lack of faith. He often depends on crowds and music and other aids, not to call out faith, but to increase suggestibility; and his removal, in a few cases, of a symptom can do untold harm to the patient. On the other hand if the patient is not cured, harm is done to him also. His depression is increased. He makes one or all of many false deductions such as that religion is no good, or Pastor X is a lying cheat, or, pathetically, that his own faith is weak, or that God has favourites.

I would remind the reader of an experience of Dr Garbett, late Archbishop of York, when he was Bishop of Southwark. There came into the diocese a 'healer' who attracted vast crowds and many professed that they were cured. The clergy approached the bishop and pressed him to let the healer come to the cathedral. Why should *they* and *their* people not have a share in the good times? Much was said of the Spirit of God being poured out. The bishop refused his permission and was much criticized. He tells us that he was comforted when, three weeks later, those healed in the first week of the mission were angrily returning to ask why their symptoms had returned or else been replaced by more distressing symptoms. [21]

[21] The Archbishop of York, Dr Cyril Garbett, addressing convocation in the autumn of 1952 (Reported in the *Manchester Guardian*).

Further, the permanent gains of healing-missions, and frequently even the temporary gains, are often negligible. The *Birkenhead News* of 10th June 1939 alleged that at a mission in Liverpool attended by thousands, not a single cure was even claimed. Any good hospital, if it chose, could give far better evidence of healing ability than is claimed even by the most plausible and enthusiastic of mission-healers.

I have myself followed up many of these missions and the claims of the missioners, and it is sad work indeed. After the publication of one dramatic alleged cure of cancer claimed by a well-known healer I made inquiry from a friend of mine in the same city who laconically sent me the Press report of the funeral service of the patient! In the West of England I was told of one heart patient who was exhorted by a healer to have faith and get up and do her housework. Though she was suffering from a coronary thrombosis she did so, stung by the charge that she had no faith; whereupon, so I was informed, she fell down dead.

Let me recapitulate some of the dangers of the healing-mission.

(1) The emotional excitement may remove a symptom, and this is falsely called a cure.
(2) The original symptom either soon returns or is replaced by one harder to cure.
(3) The disappointment of the unhealed patient leads him to make false deductions—e.g. that he has not sufficient faith when no amount of faith would have cured him, that God has favourites, that religion is no good. Another difficulty is a patient's way of confusing faith and suggestibility.
(4) The idea a patient may get that God is a means and his health the end, and that prayer and faith are in the same category as ointments and drugs, i.e. means of getting well, God being the means and the patient the end.
(5) The real danger of delaying medical and surgical help while waiting for a healer or healing-service to come along, or of supposing that it is a superior quality of faith to trust a 'healer' than a qualified physician.
(6) The lack of discrimination on the part of healers who joyously accept as patients people whom our Lord Himself would not have attempted to heal—e.g. patients with the mechanism of recovery absent, such as blind people whose eyes have been removed.

(7) The way in which the onus of 'having faith' is put wholly on the patient. In many a mission the healer takes the credit of the cures. Where he fails he implies, or even says, that the failure is due to the lack of faith on the part of the patient. Heads the healer wins; tails the patient loses.

I am aware that the way in which our Lord healed people in the street, and apparently when crowds were present, seems to present a case in favour of healing-services, but I would claim that there are important differences.

(1) 'He knew what was in man.' He could select in the crowds those whom He knew He could benefit. I am convinced that He who told a parable in which a patient was succoured by 'pouring in oil and wine' did not despise medical methods or think them unnecessary, and that He would agree that certain cases are not suitable for what is loosely called 'spiritual healing'. He would know what these were. The modern 'healer' does not. If *every illness* could be cured by 'faith' or the laying on of hands, then medical research and treatments are irrelevant. Men need no longer search for the causes of human ills or seek to prevent them, a statement which, from St Luke the physician downwards, I think all sensible Christians would say is nonsense. Again and again Christ asserted His preference for privacy and the concealment of cures, which is the very opposite of the aims of most healers. 'See thou tell no man' seems to have expressed His wish.[22]

(2) Another point to remember is that Christ did not advertise beforehand 'a healing-service'. He seems often to have moved on from one place to another just because the marvels He did in the field of healing interfered with His getting across to people the far more important message of God's kingdom, its nature and its nearness. People rushed Him and turned His attempts to preach into displays of healing power, and His great compassion would not allow Him to say them nay. But these situations are very different from healing services in modern days advertised for weeks beforehand. One cannot avoid the conclusion that though the health of the body was a much to be desired thing, it was less important to Christ than the right relationship of the soul with God, and indeed, in those cases which must have most concerned our Lord,

[22] Matthew 8^4, 9^{30}, 16^{20}, Mark 5^{43}, $7^{24,36}$, 8^{30}, 9^9, Luke 5^{14}.

renewed health was dependent on that relationship and a by-product of it. A service whose aim was the removal of a purely physical disability does not seem to me to fit at all into the New Testament picture of Christ's activities.

I therefore entirely approve of Section II in the Report issued by the Sub-Committee of the Lambeth Conference of 1920 which reads: 'On account of the immense importance that we attach to the spiritual preparation of the individual, as well as for other reasons, we are not prepared to give any encouragement to public missions of healing.'

The Public Laying-on-of-Hands

When we turn to the laying on of hands, I differentiate from the healing mission as follows:

I assume that the priest or minister has had one or more private interviews with the patient and tried to explain to him the theology that lies behind the ceremony of laying-on-of-hands. It is hard to put this briefly, and indeed, many interviews could be taken in explaining it.

My own view is that illness is never God's will in the sense of being something that God desires. No great creative artist would *desire* imperfection in the created object. The *perfect* will of God is perfect health of body, mind, and spirit. Jesus went about doing God's will. For Him, disease was the work of Satan (Luke 13[16]), and whatever we think about 'devils', the fact that He 'cast them out' shows that He thought of them as evil.

In other words, I myself say to patients: 'God wants you to be well, and He is working with your doctor and your praying friends and me to make you well.

'At the same time, belonging to the human family means not only that you have at your disposal all the assets of the family—like the knowledge and skill of doctors—but the liabilities of the family—ignorance and folly and sin. We suffer for what others have done and for what they are, and sometimes for what we ourselves have done and are. But the loving, forgiving God is ever at work to teach and restore us to unity with Him, and to that perfect health which is sometimes a by-product of that unity.

'It may be,' I say to the patient, 'that you are out of harmony with God at some point and that your illness is partly caused by that. I want you to tell me your sins and fears, your resentments and hates, your worries and guilt, and let's open it all out, and look at it quietly together and decide what can be done.

'And when I lay hands on you in the name of Christ, think of it as a sacramental act by which you—having asked God's forgiveness—seek His peace and achieve harmony with Him.

'Then, not in any magical way, you may find yourself making a great stride forward in your courageous battle for health.'

I try to explain faith to a patient beforehand, pointing out that it is not tested by recovery. One can have faith without healing and healing without faith. But there must be an act of *committal to God whatever happens*, in the knowledge that even if there are stumbling-blocks in the way of present recovery, the patient and God are working together, fighting a battle for health and holiness, and that He will use even the evil, to which He is opposed, to bring about final victory in the soul and in the world, even as He made the Cross, the result of man's evil, to be at last a symbol of victory and power and of man's redemption.

In these situations, the minister should seek to work with the doctor in charge of the case and try to understand the patient's condition. The minister has a difficult task. He must never belittle the doctor's treatment or the value of scientific remedies. He must never promise cure. He must never pretend that the patient could be cured if only he had 'faith', for there is insufficient evidence for such a conclusion. He must not make the patient too expectant. Yet he must not leave the patient concluding that the minister himself does not think much good can come from the procedure. What I try to induce is the idea that the Service is a symbol of the blessing of God upon a patient who longs to be one with Him, the hope that the Service may lead to healing, but the commitment of the patient to God *whatever happens*, in the faith that if healing be deferred, for reasons beyond our present understanding, or because of hindrances which at present we do not know how to remove, God can in the end make all things work together for a good which will be found to be worth waiting for.

To such a Service,[23] only the patient and a few close and praying friends should be admitted. It is ideal that the doctor should also attend. If there is a prayer group whose members have thought things through together, their presence would help, but the Service can be carried through with only the minister present.

---

[23] An Order for such a Service is published cheaply by the Epworth Press, 25 City Road, London, E.C.4.

When all this has been said, the laying on of hands may also be carried out, not so much as a sacramental service, but as a treatment with odic force about which I have written above. 'Odicized' oil may be used. (Perhaps Christ Himself had this force to an immensely powerful degree; we do not know, but some of His miracles (e.g. Luke 13$^{10-17}$) suggest it. For us moderns, however, it seems to me best to explain odic force to a patient whose illness is thought to be suitable for such treatment and then to use it, if the patient so desires, *as a treatment*, and not to mix up a treatment with the religious service of 'laying on of hands'.

As I have explained, odic force is possessed by quite secularly minded people and is not necessarily anything to do with religion, whereas the sacramental laying on of hands is a deeply spiritual service. Both ministries may have been combined in the early Church, and may have been combined since in the ministries of men like John Maillard[24] and Jim Wilson,[25] but it seems to me better to separate the service from the treatment, even if both are used. Neither, of course, must ever be a substitute for careful medical diagnosis and the subsequent use of whatever therapy science can suggest, but it is a mistake to think of the laying on of hands as an expedient only to be resorted to when all other methods have failed to heal the patient. One can only hope that the sacramental laying on of hands after several explanatory interviews might become normal pastoral practice for all ministers of religion.

Intercession for the Sick

At the City Temple, we offered intercession for the sick for nearly a quarter of a century. If the value of this practice is to be judged by its success as a means of making sick people well, we should be obliged to discontinue it. Let me be quite honest in this matter. Usually it appears to make no appreciable difference in the physical condition of the patient.

And, of course, a moment's thought shows us that the wisdom of God lies behind this fact. During the great plague, thousands of people must have prayed that God would make their dear ones well. But if He had done so, plague would still be with us. Men would never have done careful research to find out what caused plague, and how it could be prevented, if it could be immediately cured by—as it were—putting a prayer in the slot and drawing out

[24] See his *Healing in the Name of Jesus*, pp. 20-2 (Hodder & Stoughton, 1936).
[25] See his *Healing Through the Power of Christ*, pp. 63-4 (James Clarke, 1946).

a cure. It may well be that some diseases which baffle us today stand now where plague stood then, and that prayer, though of spiritual value in maintaining morale, is not the relevant way of co-operating with God. What God *could* do is a question no one can answer. What God *does* do is a signpost we should do well to heed. God very often awaits our co-operation to fulfil His will, and if, as a human family, we spent on, say, cancer research, what we spend on manufacturing sputniks which travel round the planets, we might in this generation end the scourge of cancer as we have ended the scourge of plague. In the meantime, the individual goes on suffering, even though he has the assurance that in the end God will weave his suffering into as valuable and glorious a pattern as health could have achieved.

The Christian, however, is not to abstain from prayer because it often does not 'work'. He is commanded to make intercession for the sick, and to do so without asking what the result will be.

My own method is to offer such intercession at a public service, for there are sure to be *some* genuine Christians in a congregation who will co-operate. I first obtain permission to mention the sufferer's name, because the congregation can thereby make a better picture of the patient and his needs. I avoid too detailed a description of his sufferings or too gloomy a prognosis. I explain that we are not telling God something He does not know, or persuading a reluctant God to 'intervene'. We are gladly co-operating with a willing God, just as the conscientious nurse or doctor does. All healing is of God, and as the nurses and doctors co-operate on the physical plane, so we, by prayer, 'lending our minds to God' as the doctors and nurses lend their skill, co-operate on psychic and spiritual levels. If we can surround the deep mind of the patient with *our* optimism, buoyancy, faith and trust, then our caring may alter the environment of the patient's deep mind, just as an oxygen tent or a dressing alters the environment of a sick part of his body. And if a patient exchanges, though it be unconsciously, defeat and despair and pessimism for courage and the will to live, then he has a better chance of recovery. Sometimes we seem to be rewarded with marvellous results. In other cases, the patient does not feel physically better but is improved mentally and spiritually. In still other cases the patient dies, but he dies in peace feeling that all is well and that a wonderful life is opening before him.

I must record one 'result' which to me is very striking. Prayer is followed by recovery comparatively frequently in cases where the

PRESENT-DAY NON-MEDICAL METHODS OF HEALING 59

patient is a child. I imagine that this is because an adult mind is walled up, even down to a deep level, against the invasion of ideas. I must admit that if three specialists said I was suffering from an incurable illness and had only a few weeks to live, I should find it very difficult by faith and trust in God to believe that they were wrong and that I should recover through the power released through prayer.

But the mind of a little child is not thus walled up. It is open to the invasion of ideas from outside itself even at a deep level. A child does not decide—'I cannot get better'. He probably does not meditate at all on his condition, or accept gloomy prognoses. Peoples' prayers and their loving, their caring and longing, winged to him by sincere prayer, probably penetrate his deep mind and increase its resilience and its resistance to disease. At any rate, the facts seem to support this, though, of course, children recover more rapidly than adults in any circumstance.

To offer an unexpectant prayer like 'God bless all who are sick and make them well' may be futile. In fact, little is hoped for. One recovery would astonish the intercessor! But to lift up in prayer a known and loved person, to imagine Christ standing by his bedside and more able to succour because of our caring, to co-operate with God's willingness and join in the fight for health which He inspires, seems to me part of the Christian's duty and privilege.

The rare occasions when healing follows and *seems* to be due to prayer should be relentlessly examined. Prayer must also be within the realm of law, and though faith compels us to continue, understanding would help us to be more effective, and to be able to guard men from bitter disappointment when prayer does not bring them the health they crave.

4

THE MINISTER AND PRIVATE METHODS

The Place of Confession[26]

IN my opinion, Free Church people ought to have at the hands of their ministers all that is of value in the Roman confessional. They ought to have ready access to a minister who makes time to listen, who is skilled in counselling, who has intuitive insight into human

---

[26] I have written more fully on Confession in *Psychology in Service of the Soul*, pp. 78ff (Epworth Press), and in *Psychology, Religion and Healing*, pp. 337ff and 447ff (Hodder & Stoughton).

problems, and who can keep the confidences of those who come to him, not sharing them even with his own wife or with the patient's relatives.

Rome has made confession habitual when it should be occasional and even rare, compulsory when it should be voluntary, and mechanical when it should be spontaneous. I would extend the idea of the confessional so that not only sins but worries, fears, sorrows, anxieties and phobias are exteriorized by recital.

Very many people have suffered all sorts of ills of body and mind who could have been delivered if they had had some sympathetic, understanding friend to whom they could have poured out their troubles.

I think of a boy who suffered agonies at boarding-school because he was told that masturbation was not only a terrible sin but would bring on insanity. He believed—having been told by an adult whom he trusted—that the fluid which escaped from his body was the actual substance of his brain! One sentence from another friend ended his troubles at once, but he was on the way to severe neurosis with physical symptoms.

I think of a woman of fifty who still suffers because of the teachings given her in her childhood about hell and the imminence of our Lord's return. In terror she nightly tried to be 'ready for His appearing', and tried to keep awake, feeling terribly guilty when sleep overtook her.

In his book, *A Mind that Found Itself*, C. W. Beers tells us that he tried to commit suicide by throwing himself from an upper window because his brother had epilepsy and he was told that it was infectious and that he would catch it. He became convinced that he had already caught it, and that the attacks were being concealed from him. One sentence from an adequate authority would have saved him ten years' misery, but he never confided his fears to anyone.

People are afraid they will be laughed at, or disapproved of, or called silly and fanciful, and so they keep their fears to themselves.

> *Give sorrow words, the grief that does not speak*
> *Whispers the o'er fraught heart and bids it break.*[27]

This is true, not only of sorrow but of secret dreads, and it is true not only of adults but of children. I was told of one home where,

[27] *Macbeth*, IV.iii.

when their father died, three children were sent away from home to shield them from the grief of relatives at the funeral, and from their mother's tears. All three developed neurosis, and some of them physical symptoms, because, taking counsel only with one another, they concluded that their mother had murdered their father and wanted them out of the way. By the time they discovered the truth, they were on the way to being chronic neurotics. Grief would have done them far less harm.

I have treated a large number of people who have only needed 'a listening ear and an understanding heart' for their symptoms to disappear. One lady recently suffered agonies of mental unhappiness because on a holiday abroad her husband developed a passion for visiting Roman Catholic churches and she found that the almost nude figure of Christ on the many crucifixes aroused in her starved nature sexual feelings which she thought were not only wicked but blasphemous. She never told her husband about it. He was a most understanding man and could have quietened her fears, eased her distress and given her the sexual satisfaction the need of which was so clearly indicated. She made up a story that the churches were stuffy, so, for hours in inexpressible misery, she sat alone in the car while her disappointed husband tried to enjoy his holiday largely by himself.

Such people, and the comparative ease with which some of them are cured, remind me of the passage in Dr T. A. Ross's book *The Common Neuroses* where he says: 'His case needed only free discussion for the symptoms to be dissipated.'[28]

It will certainly be asked why it is not enough to make confession to God direct, to pour out to Him in prayer those things which worry and affright us. Surely the answer is that it *is* enough if God is real enough for us to *feel* that our outpouring is real. The truth is that God for most of us is remote and unreal, and we need a human friend who makes the confession at once costly but cathartic.

If we listen to such confessions we shall find many interesting features about them.

(1) People will confess mere peccadilloes. Care must be taken here in two ways: (*a*) The so-called peccadillo may not be

---

[28] (Arnold 1924), p. 142. The way in which confession disperses physical symptoms is well illustrated in *The Way of Release*, by Dr Ernest White of Harley Street, a member of the staff of the City Temple Psychological Clinic (published by Marshall, Morgan & Scott).

trifling to the person who confesses it. Much depends on his upbringing, his ideals and his sense of values, and the confessor must never treat lightly what the penitent feels is heinous. (b) But it must be recognized that the confession of a trifle often masks the withholding of something serious. I well remember a man telling me in tears, that having obtained petrol during war time for professional purposes he had used it to go on a holiday. He withheld the fact that during the holiday he had raped a girl staying in the same hotel. 'When we dare not acknowledge some great sin,' said Jung, 'we deplore some small sin with greater emphasis.'

(2) At the same time, we shall find in some patients a technical 'scrupulosity'. Dr David Yellowlees tells of a patient of his who painted a cushion cover the design of which included a bunch of grapes. When the article was ready for sale it occurred to her that wine was made from grapes and that the purchaser might take to drink. She felt so guilty that she forthwith destroyed it.[29]

(3) It will be found that a very common reason which induces a person to make confession is the habit of masturbation. What with the taboo of secrecy about sex, coupled with the almost ineradicable idea in many minds that anything to do with sex is sin, thousands of people are made miserable by the feelings of guilt set up by this almost universal habit and many are driven by it to confession.

'Is masturbation sin?' was a question handed up to me in the pulpit one 'question night' at the City Temple. The answer I gave was that it depends on the picture on the screen of the mind when the masturbation is practised. If a young man is separated from his wife, and masturbates while phantasizing that he is having intercourse with her, I cannot feel that this is sin. He is carrying out an act which would be quite guilt-free if she were lying beside him. But if someone else's wife is in the phantasy, then I think the act is sin because he is undermining his own self-control. If, having made this phantasy many times, he found himself actually alone with the woman concerned, he might easily do in fact what he had previously done in phantasy, since the 'grooves of activity' would already have been prepared ready for the flow of passion made almost uncontrollable by the situation imagined earlier.

Usually, however, it is enough to ask the Christian patient if he

[29] *Psychology's Defence of the Faith* (SCM, 1930), p. 97.

would be content to show to our Lord the picture on the screen of his mind when masturbation takes place. Often there is no picture at all and therefore no sin. The act is a purely physical release of tension no more wicked than scratching one's head because it itches. A lady of nearly seventy wept in my room recently because —as she confessed—she succumbed to masturbation at rare intervals. I could see no harm in it at all. With young people idealizing in phantasy with imaginary lovers, masturbation is to be discouraged, because it can fixate sexual development at youthful levels, but the discouragement must not treat the habit as a terrible sin. A mother once brought her daughter of twelve to me and reported masturbation. When I asked the mother what she had done about it I found she had hidden herself in her daughter's bedroom, and when she suspected that the child was masturbating she leapt out, drew back the bedclothes, stripped the child naked and thrashed her with a cane. Anything more likely to cause lifelong neurosis and unhappy marriage it is hard to imagine. When a father brought his young son to me and in the boy's presence asked me to tell the boy the 'terrible results of masturbation' I felt incensed enough to turn on the father and say: 'Well, it doesn't seem to have done you much harm, does it?'

Actually the habit, unless worried about, does no harm at all, but it repeatedly comes up in 'the confessional' and usually one can assess the degree of sinfulness in it. If it is sin, we can offer the loving forgiveness of God and the new, clean start. More often, we can unburden a mind and lift a load of guilt which should never have been carried.

It remains to write a little on the attitude of the minister to psychiatric treatment. Here I hope I shall be forgiven if I am autobiographical.

For reasons and in circumstances into which I need not enter, I began to take an interest in the relevance of psychology to my job as a minister at the end of World War I. In those days 'the new psychology' was very new indeed. Books by Tansley, Crichton-Miller, and Pym poured from the Press and the work of J. A. Hadfield, particularly his *Psychology and Morals* and his essay in *The Spirit* on 'The Psychology of Power', thrilled many of us young ministers. We eagerly studied all we could lay hands on and discussed the matter in groups.

When I returned to England in 1922 I began to try to use my

new knowledge in my pastoral work, and I was lucky enough to meet with some startling successes. It should be remembered that at this time psychology was not even included in the curriculum of the medical student, though it was in that of the ministerial students. The doctors who now say to ministers 'This is nothing to do with you' should remember that the doctors used to say 'This is nothing to do with us'. The word 'psychiatry' was not born. Neuroses were called 'nerves' ('The doctor says it's my nerves'), and the *only* treatment was bromide, rest and holidays.

I found, to my delight, that by putting a patient under hypnosis I could trace back a condition to its originating incident or group of incidents, and by getting the patient later to the state of conscious acceptance of such origins, or by letting him feel again and 'explode' the emotion connected therewith, I could sometimes make the lame walk and the deaf hear, and so on. We are now all familiar with these psychosomatic diseases, but recognition of them and treatment of them psychologically was very rare in the 1920's.

I wish to emphasize here that if I, and those like me, including a very few greatly suspected doctors like Hadfield who himself had been a minister, had not attempted to help people suffering in this way, they would have remained unhelped.

Gradually, when I was a minister in Leeds (1925-36), I built up a co-operating relationship with one or two doctors. I shall never forget the thrill I felt when Prof. Maxwell Telling, then Professor of Medicine in the University of Leeds, asked me to undertake the case of a patient of his, a young girl in his nursing-home, whose terror caused her so to shake that the things on her dressing-table rattled with her shaking. I saw her more than seventy times, after which she recovered enough to drive her car about Leeds and take up her work again in another Yorkshire city. Dr Telling took one real risk in that act of co-operation, and another when he kindly wrote a preface to my book *Psychology in Service of the Soul*. When an Oxford professor brought his own wife to see me in Leeds, and to stay there for treatment, I began to feel that the ground under my feet was not quite so dangerously slippery, though I was regarded by many ministers and doctors with the lifted eyebrow and with many expressions of criticism.

When I went in 1936 to the City Temple, London, I established there the 'City Temple Psychological Clinic'. We tried to focus on needy people the energies released by Religion, Medicine and

Psychology, and at one time I could call on twelve medically qualified Christian men and women with either psychological training, or insight based on their own analysis. That work, I am glad to say, still goes on, and I still take part in it.

But now things are different. I should not now *attempt* some of the things I did a quarter of a century ago. Immense progress has been made in psychiatry. At one time an intelligent minister could not only keep up with what the doctors were doing (they were called then 'psychotherapists') but he was in the van of leadership and knew his Freud, Jung and Adler better than most general practitioners in medicine. Freud himself had expressed a preference that ministers rather than doctors should take up his work. His words are worth recalling. 'It may be asked whether the practice of psychoanalysis does not presuppose a medical education which must remain lacking to the educator and pastor, or whether other relations are not antagonistic to the purpose of placing the psychoanalytic technique in other than medical hands. I confess that I see no such obstacles. The practice of psychoanalysis depends much less on medical education than psychological preparation and free human insight; the majority of physicians, however, are not fitted for the practice of psychoanalysis, and have completely failed in placing a correct valuation on this method of treatment. The educator and pastor are bound by the demands of their vocations to exercise the same consideration, forbearance, and restraint which the physician is accustomed to observe, and their being habitually associated with youth makes them perhaps better suited to have a sympathetic insight into the mental life of this class of persons. The guarantee for a harmless application of the psychoanalytic method can, however, only be afforded in both cases by the personality of the analyst.'[30]

Nowadays, there are scores of medically qualified psychiatrists, and furthermore, the minister cannot hope to keep up with their methods. Hypnosis, though it still has an important place in treatment, has largely given way to drugs, which, of course, the minister is not qualified to use. Electro-convulsive therapy (E.C.T.) is applied to patients so as to get quick results where in old days we sat down day after day for hours patiently listening and trying to fathom the causes of the patient's depression. Brain surgery (prefrontal leucotomy) is now resorted to where we could only try to help the patient to live with his disability.

[30] Introduction to *The Psychoanalytic Method*, by Oskar Pfister, p. 7.

Where then does the minister stand? Should he stand right away from these wounded spirits save to refer them to medically qualified psychiatrists, preferably those who are themselves Christians?

My own view is that though he will do less and less in the field of treatment, co-operation as we practise it at the City Temple is still an ideal which would be extremely valuable if widely followed.

Let me set out what a minister can do when a neurotic patient comes to him.

(1) He can be a good minister. I mean by that that he can talk to the patient about God, showing him that God loves and cares and is fighting with the patient and the doctors to restore health. When the patient reveals that his theology is faulty (e.g. that he thinks his sickness is the will of God, or that he is being punished by God) the minister can try to remedy it, and when the patient reveals that his faith is weak, the minister can try to 'build him up in our most holy faith'. Many a patient is really eager to talk with a minister, not about psychology but about his sins, and about God, and about God's ways with men.

(2) He can refer the patient to a psychiatrist who is capable and sympathetic and who will not deride or undermine the patient's religious beliefs, and, while the treatment proceeds, the minister can give immense help both to the psychiatrist and patient by seeing the latter from time to time and giving him assurance and encouragement. To many patients repeated treatments are still strange and bewildering.

(3) He can, with the patient's permission, discuss the case with the psychiatrist. If the latter finds that a sense of guilt lies underneath the neurosis, the minister can see the patient for a number of sessions aimed at getting the patient to receive the transforming gift of God's forgiveness.

(4) If—as surely should be true—the minister is in touch with a loving group of *really* Christian people, he can introduce the patient to a suitable group. Again and again group-therapy has proved efficacious. The patient is received and loved and accepted and approved, and meets others who possibly have passed through the deep valley of neurosis and found the way out. Nothing more encourages the neurotic than fellowship with one who can say: 'Yes, I know just how you feel. I felt like that once. You will come through as I did.'

(5) The minister must never pretend to a knowledge he does not possess, but there are still some situations in which, if the minister does not try to help, the patient remains unhelped. There are still country people for instance who have no chance of the help of a medical psychiatrist. Apart from the problem of distance it is regrettable that some psychiatrists will charge from eight to ten guineas for a single interview, and if the patient claims out-patient help through the NHS he will be kept waiting for weeks and then perhaps get twenty minutes once a week—a completely farcical way of pretending to meet his need. A minister can do a great deal of good merely by listening.

(6) I was enheartened to read the printed duties of the chaplains in at least one of our great London hospitals: 'To visit and make himself acquainted with the patients and with their spiritual difficulties and to collaborate with the Medical Staff under the direction of the Medical Superintendent in cases where it appears he can assist in restoring a patient's mental and spiritual health.' The chaplain has a weekly meeting with the Medical Superintendent and cases are commended to his care both then and through individual doctors. The chaplain has full access to case sheets in which mention may be made of religious factors. It is generally agreed by the medical staff that the chaplain can help most, either when the patient first comes into hospital, or after the medical treatment is concluded.

(7) Let us not forget the therapeutic value of preaching. We now realize how many physical illnesses are touched off and overlong continued because in the deep mind some emotion inimical to health is being retained. Men develop ulcers and coronary thromboses because of worry. They have headaches because of fear. They have arthritic conditions made worse by resentments. They have epileptic fits—or so they are often diagnosed—through repressed hate. And guilt can be a potent cause of all kind of illnesses. A patient develops sometimes a skin disease because his spirit is irritated. He maintains asthma or migraine or even a bad cold because he is starved of love. If, then, in a church service a man exchanges guilt for forgiveness, if he lets go of resentment or jealousy or anger or envy and begins to love his brother man, if he substitutes trust in God for worry, and so on, then in the field of

preventive medicine alone, the chaplain or minister has done a great thing for him.

(8) The minister has one great opportunity which he should try not to miss. He is the only professional person who has entry to a home without being summoned. If equipped with some psychological insight and a real love of his people, he can often spot neurotic situations before they land people in neurosis. The young male lodger who is slowly getting emotionally entangled with his young landlady; the first child of a marriage being pushed into inferiority by a younger arrival; the ordinary sensitive child pushed into inferiority by a brilliant brother or sister; the 'in-laws' who stay too long; the 'granny' who makes bringing up a child so difficult; the daughter who, frankly, hates her mother and dare not show it; the elderly man, mentally, if not physically, unfaithful to his wife—all these give scope to the minister who has enough friendship, authority, insight and tact to deal with these situations before neurosis sets in, or who, ideally supported by a co-operating doctor, dare insist on breaking up some situations even after neurosis has shown itself.

In another place I have quoted the opinions of many psychiatrists about the value of religion in the field of psychiatry[31]. I should like to quote here the words written since by no less an authority than Jung. Writing to the Rev. George C. Anderson, Executive Secretary of the National Academy of Religion and Mental Health, New York, on 14th April, 1956, Dr Jung said: 'I have long felt the need of theologians and psychiatrists collaborating in the field of Mental Hygiene and Psychotherapy of Neuroses. Indeed, I have urged already in 1932 at a Pastoral Conference in Strassburg that such a pooling of ideas is a primary necessity. Religious resources together with psychological knowledge and insight would furnish an illuminated approach towards the solving of many problems of Modern Man.'

In conclusion, I have obtained permission to quote the words of my friend, the Rev. Erastus Evans, M.A., from his excellent book *Pastoral Care in a Changing World*.[32]

'The Pastor sees the sick person in his crisis before God. He lives through it with him in a way that seeks to establish a

---

[31] See *Psychology, Religion and Healing*, p. 476.
[32] Epworth Press, p. 92.

permanent meaning for it in the sufferer's relation with God. This is an integral part of healing. But human situations are not always amenable to human endeavour, whether that of the Pastor or the medical man. Indeed in the final sense the human situation is not amenable to human control, and we are confronted with ultimate mysteries, such as incurable disease, madness, and death. There comes a point where the scientific healer can do no more, and in a certain sense has departed from the need, although he continues to care for the patient, and to do the few little things that are still physically possible. The Pastor's vocation requires that he should still stay. When the psychiatric treatment has failed and the patient has committed suicide, the Pastor is there among the relatives facing insoluble problems, trying to turn bitterness towards God and life into softness and compassion for the human lot. He sits down beside the incurable to whom science can offer no alleviation or hope and whom medical treatment has to pass by, as beside one infinitely precious to God. He talks to the mentally sick although what he says does not seem to penetrate into his lonely and crazed world. He prays beside the dying who lies in a coma and has already cast off the moorings of this world. If the Pastor proclaims a hope that is not of this life, he must often stand silent before the hopelessness of this world. He must often feel as ineffective as the disciples watching the crucified Saviour, powerless to remove Him from the Cross. But still he stays. It is his vocation to stand by crucified humanity; he stays as he would at the foot of the Cross. The writer remembers the cry of a young widow who had been suddenly and terribly bereaved of her husband, and was at last able to think of her experience: "You were there!" There is meaning in the Pastor's presence, even though, from the scientific standpoint, he may have been regarded as useless.'

4
The Significance of the New Testament Healing Miracles for the Modern Healer

Erastus Evans

THE SIGNIFICANCE OF THE NEW TESTAMENT HEALING MIRACLES FOR THE MODERN HEALER

THE PHILOSOPHICAL AND THE RELIGIOUS APPROACH TO NEW TESTAMENT MIRACLES

IT IS NOT our intention in this essay to define 'miracle' and to go into the question of 'the miraculous' as such. It is impossible to find a satisfactory definition of 'miracle'. If it is defined as 'contravention of natural law', the question immediately arises as to our knowledge of such a supposed law. In spite of our knowledge of its processes, this remains a mysterious universe.

Something may appear to be in defiance of natural law in A.D. 1800 which is seen to be scientifically explicable in A.D. 1962. The definition mentioned implies a closed system of nature about which everything is known. But this implication only has to be stated in order to see that it is impossible to claim such a knowledge. The Christian is not concerned with the scientific definition of miracle. He is concerned with miracle as a religious value. New Testament writers had no scientific sense in the way a modern man has. They knew nothing about a closed system of nature. Such a conception belongs to the eighteenth rather than the first century. In fact, the ancient world was prepared to accept things far more incredible than the miracles of the New Testament. The Bible writers are concerned with God's dealings with men. It is not the contravention of nature, as such, which interests them, but the conviction that God has acted in certain specific events, and that He can be experienced in His power and mercy there.

It does not really matter to the Christian man whether a providential event can be scientifically explained at some immediate or more remote time. In spite of the explanation it may still be to him an action of God as far as he is concerned. If my life is spared in an operation during which all the doctors expected me to die, it matters little if the scientific fact be discovered at some future time which explains this. Before the operation I was within, as it were, a closed system in which everything indicated the impossibility of my ever surviving it. It was impossible to know then that I would be spared. As a religious man I may regard my survival as a special mercy of God towards me. If no further information about it were forthcoming I might be justified in using the word 'miracle' about it. But even if it were explained, the special mercy of God towards me is not minimized thereby. It is not the fact that the healing miracles of the New Testament defy all medical analysis that is important. They are seen within the framework of the Kingdom of God, as manifestations of the power and love of God in our Lord Jesus Christ. Whatever rationalizing explanations may come in future generations with regard to them, they need not minimize the revelationary power that is within them. They still speak of a spirit of love and a power to do good to men, and they still testify to the fact that God's knowledge is far beyond ours. Where we see closed doors, He is able to open them and to act in freedom.

MIRACLE AS SYMBOL

In the New Testament a miracle is not only an event, it is also a symbol. The shifting of the terminology testifies to this. The 'wonders' of the Synoptics become 'signs' in the Gospel of John. Astonishment at the events grows into a sense of their revelatory power. They become 'signs' which indicate something of the depth of life which is revealed in Jesus. They become tokens of something far deeper in life, which they indicate but do not exhaust. They are seen to be symbolic.

Their symbolic significance was not artificially invented for them in the manner that the three crosses of the Union Jack were combined in order to symbolize Britain. They were intrinsically and inherently symbolic, symbolic in their very happening. They were not a shorthand conveying technical information as to how wonderful healings could be achieved. The miracles of the New Testament became symbolic by a far deeper process. The depths of life spoke to man's superficial life by their means. They symbolize a divine mercy which broods over human life and is prepared to enter when it finds faith and courage. They symbolize the divine dimension to life which is the source of renewing power. They symbolize the fact that life is always open as far as God is concerned, that the present and past need never control the future, and that faith can experience this openness. They are a testimony against the closed minds of men.

Without a belief in the miracles of faith, man would remain imprisoned in his conceptions of the possible. This statement is not to be interpreted pietistically, as though it were merely a declaration in favour of the orthodox. Faith is a fundamental human activity and necessity, and it can be present in the scientist while engaged in his scientific work. Fact is not the only element in science. Venture, courage, faith, in the deep human sense, are an integral part of its activity, without which it could not advance. The faith-healer's claim to monopolize faith is unwarranted. The testimony against the tyranny of the closed system, the apparent only possibility, is necessary in every human sphere.

THE INCARNATION AND HISTORY

Christian faith sees Jesus as unique, as the one man in whom God is manifest. It must be emphasized, however, that God is found precisely in the humanity of Jesus. The Incarnation is not to be confused with the appearance of a demigod, who was in reality immune from human limitations and could transcend them at will. Such a creature would be in reality neither God nor man. He would never be capable of showing the love of God taking on human limitation, nor would he truly experience what it is to be man, which surely implies a limitation of knowledge and power. He would be immune from the human problem. He would be so superior to man, and so essentially different, that the only possibility left to human beings would be an unquestioning obedience to an overwhelming power. The rejection of the Temptations in the wilderness shows that Jesus did not regard Himself in this way.

The uniqueness of Jesus does not mean that He was independent of history, and not subject to its relativity in any way. We cannot consider the healing miracles of Jesus completely apart from the notions of His own time about disease, or in unawareness of the mental climate of His age. If the Incarnation was real, it happened in the midst of these, and was necessarily coloured by them, and manifested itself in reactions that occurred in such an environment. We read the New Testament in order that we may come to understand the revelation of God which it contains. The sincere reader is confronted with God in the words and deeds of Jesus, but this is by no means a stiff, wooden and arbitrary matter. Jesus appears to us through the veil of history, and the story about Him is conveyed through the fragmentariness of the records, and bears upon it the stamp of a particular age and environment and way of thought. Thus when we consider the healing miracles of Jesus, we are not only concerned with the understanding of God, and under judgement from the beyond, but in this very study two ages are meeting, that of the apostles and our own. It is most important for us not to confuse these two aspects of the matter.

REALITY OF THE TENSION BETWEEN THE NEW TESTAMENT AND THE MODERN HEALER

There are those for whom everything in the New Testament remains normative and sacrosanct, so that not only the knowledge of God which comes to us from this source, but also every practice and thought within it must be scrupulously copied with no deviation. Thus, for example, the rabbinical demonology of the New Testament is accepted without question by some, in spite of the fact that it is not peculiar to the New Testament, and that modern medicine has proved that causes other than demons are operative in the spreading of disease, and that there are effective ways of dealing with a fever besides addressing it as though it were a demon.[1]

Such people ignore the real issue with regard to the help that the New Testament can give to the modern healer. We must ask: 'What is really Christian in the attitude of the New Testament to disease, and what may be regarded as the common practice of the time, or something that is part of its mental climate?' We cannot avoid the fact that two ages meet when we approach the New Testament on this matter, the pre-scientific age in which it was written, and our own scientific time. This does not mean that we simply adopt a superior attitude and regard everything the New Testament says about healing as naïve; in fundamental matters we shall always be the learners; but we must keep our feet firmly in our own age. We cannot avoid taking up a questioning and not merely an accepting attitude. We must not simply give up our modern points of view and surrender our minds to the New Testament in everything. Neither must we assume that there is

[1] Luke 4^{39}: '(Jesus) *rebuked* the fever.'

nothing more to be learned. This would be just modern vanity. A real dialectic between the New Testament and the modern healer could be most fruitful. It should show where the real inspiration of the New Testament lies for the modern healer; it should save him from mere superstitious acceptance, out of religious reverence, of what is no longer relevant, and set him free to pursue healing in his modern setting with new insight.

The unprofitable attempt to define miracle, and to think of miracles as a contravention of natural law, long prevented a simpler approach to them to see what they mean for religion and for the man who longs to aid his fellows.

CHANGING ASPECTS OF THIS TENSION

There was a time when miracles were the mainstay of Christian apologetic. Their presence in the New Testament was the proof of its divine authority. This unquestioning acceptance was characteristic of the Middle Ages and did not alter with the Reformation. It was with the Enlightenment of the eighteenth century that a critical attitude arose. Miracles began to be not so much a proof of divine authority as a source of embarrassment to apologists. They became incredible to the intellectuals, and there was a tendency to reject them entirely. This was a reflection of the confidence of the science of the time which imagined that it was discovering a fixed order of nature from which there could be no departures. The ensuing controversies of the nineteenth century, for the most part, did little good to religion, although the sometimes stupid efforts of the orthodox to stem the rising tide of scientific criticism were at least a testimony against a closed human system which believed it was exhausting the knowledge of what was possible and impossible. However, the very advance of science provided an antidote to the attitude which rejected the New Testament miracles. The closed systems of scientific thought were themselves destroyed by this advance.

We now live in a world in which all things are possible; the older scientific dogmatism has gone. In particular the growth of psychological knowledge has made the credibility of many of the miracles apparent. The connection between skin disease and emotional disorder has made the speedy healing of leprosy intelligible, if the term 'leper' was used in the New Testament (as we have reason to believe) in a wider sense which covered many skin disorders. Psychiatrists are able to report sudden healings of the apparently paralysed which are similar to the Gospel miracle. Psychosomatic medicine has unexpectedly come to the support of the Gospel story.

This does not mean, however, that criticism can be abandoned. The tension between a scientific and a pre-scientific age is not thereby lessened. The modern doctor finds in the Gospel no scientific diagnosis and no aftercare to show that the cures were permanent. The element of exaggeration is plainly there in the stories: the cure of one blind man quickly becomes the cure of two blind men, although the form of the story shows that the same incident is being recorded.[2] The naïveté that regards being stunned as equivalent to being dead can be seen in the story of Eutychus (Acts 20^{7ff}). Sheer ignorance of the real nature of the kind of snake concerned probably accounts for the miraculous invulnerability of Paul (Acts 28^{3ff}). Primitive people have often an exaggerated notion of the harmfulness of certain snakes. There is no doubt that we are in a simple and unsophisticated mental climate when reading the New Testament.

Here it is to be noted that historical sense comes to aid us as we read of the healing miracles. This does not mean that we carefully amass evidence to prove that something called a 'miracle', regarded as a contravention of natural law, occurred, and that this can be historically proved. We have already seen that such a proof by its very definition is impossible. We do see, however, on every page of the New Testament story that Christ's deeds transcended men's expectations and thoughts. They 'never saw it on this wise' (Mk 2^{12}). These deeds revealed God to them. What is manifest in the New Testament is the way in which Jesus impressed His day and generation. The important question is not whether Jesus was consciously contravening every possible formulation of scientific law. Such a person appearing in the first century would have been a monstrosity and not a human being; the New Testament does not speak of contraventions of natural law, but of 'wonders' and 'signs'. A new life and a new kind of man had appeared in the world. Exorcisms and cures were wrought by others as well as by Jesus: 'By whom do your sons cast them out?' (Mt 12^{27}). The important thing is to contemplate the new spirit in which they were wrought, the characteristics which distinguished them from other healings of the time.

[2] Compare Mark 10^{46ff} with Matthew 20^{29ff}.

THE SIGNIFICANCE OF THE N.T. HEALING MIRACLES 77

The barren philosophical question as to the nature of a miracle should be set aside in favour of a historical intuition as to how the people of His time felt about Jesus. The revelatory power is not in the philosophy, but in the new life and spirit which infuses these deeds of Jesus. The simple religious approach which asks what Jesus's intervention meant to the people of His time, and what His deeds conveyed to them, will bring more understanding of the value of His healing miracles to the modern than any attempt to prove that they are forever scientifically inexplicable.

GAINS TO BE WON FROM THE TENSION

The critical tension between the outlook of the New Testament and that of our own time, while it seems superficially to deprive us of a norm and an authority, is in its essence productive of great good. The New Testament was not given us to destroy human initiative and creativity. It did not provide us with a technique of healing which will be valid for all time; if it had tried to do so, it could say nothing impressive to an age which far transcends it in such matters. It is not that its techniques are different from our own which makes the New Testament important to the modern healer. Very little is said about the technique of healing in the New Testament and what does appear there is of little medical value. No one is likely today to regard spittle and clay as a means of opening the eyes of the blind (Jn 9^6), or oil as having healing properties in itself, simply because it is recommended for the healing rite by the New Testament (Jas 5^{14}, Lk 10^{34}). Modern man must analyse the oil and know its properties. Holiness is not enough for him; he must have scientific information. It is not possible simply to adopt the technique of Jesus in dealing with the demoniacs and assume that it applies to every poor soul who suffers from mental delusions and schizophrenia today. A Harley Street psychiatrist would find his methods of healing of little value in facing a Bush African who believed that he had been bewitched, unless the analyst were prepared to put aside his civilized techniques. This would be because the mental climate and 'systems of reference' of the two would be quite different. So the world of Jesus's day and our own are separate, and the techniques of the one are not those of the other. In any case, before we adopted Jesus's technique we should have to ask if it differed from that of the Rabbis of the time, for we should not have the least Christian obligation to adopt their methods.

Technique is not the vital matter for the modern person who reads the New Testament stories of healing. It is what he learns there about the essential nature of man that is important to him. It is the setting in which healing appears and the large and revolutionary conception of healing which are important. It is good for him to struggle with the New Testament on these issues. If he finds it easy to put the New Testament right on points of technique, it may well be that the New Testament may challenge his whole approach to healing and his conception of the patient with whom he deals. While he finds it simple to deal with the human and transient notions of the time, he may find the very use of his drugs and psychoanalytical methods brought to a bar to which he is not accustomed. It is true that when we read the New Testament two ages are challenging each other, but it is not merely two ages which are in the encounter. The whole value and motive of human activity are tried here, and the breadth of consideration is infinitely widened. The critical questioning and the temporary rejection of the healing miracles which began with the Enlightenment may turn out ultimately to have been a cleansing process which makes it possible for the modern to face them without denying his own scientific powers, and yet with eyes freed from the unimportant and transient detail of the New Testament to consider the basic challenges with which it presents him.

The difference between the attitude of the New Testament healing and our own should make us ponder afresh what the Christian element in healing can be. Is the kind of healing portrayed there the only kind of healing that can be termed Christian, and is the practice of today, based as it is on the researches of man, at best a kind of second best, an arm of flesh that betrays its human origin?

SCIENCE AND THE WORD OF FAITH

The main difficulty for the modern healer who reads the New Testament is that the cures of the New Testament are wrought through the word of faith, and those of the modern healer are wrought by a knowledge of science. There seems to be a tension between the two methods from the very beginning. The word of faith is not dependent upon scientific knowledge. Science has achieved its present position by not taking things on trust. There are those who simply follow the New Testament and who despise scientific technique and achievement as all too human. On the other hand, a scientific method of healing is firmly established in our modern life and has proved its worth by its results. Is this tension between the two merely something superficial, and can it be in some way resolved; or is the cleavage permanent and is the truth that modern man has far transcended the atmosphere and the needs of the New Testament? Are the modern 'faith-healers' the true successors of the New Testament, and the folk who understand it best; or is 'faith-healing' an unintelligent imitation of the New Testament based on a superficial interpretation of the meaning of faith, which fails to comprehend Christianity as a developing religion?

The word of faith in the New Testament was of course something far larger than a technique of healing. It concerned the whole of man's existence and his relationship to God. Wherever it was proclaimed it meant that God was in the situation, however incurable the disease seemed to be, or however the demoniac raved. The power of God was there to help. When this word is accepted by faith, it begins to transform any situation; that it may be a complex modern situation, in which science is an element, does not fundamentally matter. It must be admitted, however, that the people of the time in which the New Testament miracles were wrought were comparatively simple and naïve. A spoken word could have more power in their midst than it could have with modern man. This can still be experienced among primitive peoples. Modern man, for good or ill, is a very different creature, and although he is still suggestible, the spoken word has not always the immediate power over him that was possible in simpler times. Nevertheless, the essence of Jesus's proclamation had nothing to do with suggestion. There was the actual contact with God, the profound realization that God's power to help reaches into every situation and makes it possible to face it with new courage.

It may be, however, that a mere naïve imitation of what Jesus was doing may miss the situation of the modern man entirely. Faith in the presence of a healing power may be just as real, but it may need to be expressed in a different way, although Jesus's supreme confidence will ever remain the symbol for every man who wishes to change a situation and to bring the power of God to aid his fellows. The epitomized form of the accounts of the miracles and the enthusiasm with which they are told must not blind us into believing that healing is an easy business. The 'much prayer' to which Jesus refers in the case of the epileptic boy and the fact that he was unable to heal in certain circumstances should convince us otherwise. A light-hearted imitation of Jesus as though a new kind of magic had been discovered is likely to miss the point in any situation. The supreme emphasis of the New Testament is that the triumphs of faith are wrought through suffering and sacrifice.

Healing problems are not solved just by repeating that it is necessary to have faith. Faith itself is a matter which needs deep examination. It may be that, when we understand the essence of faith, we shall see that it can be, as it were, 'depolarized', that it can pass from the situations of the New Testament into the modern scientific setting. In any case we are faced with the fact that scientific healing has rid the world of more disease in half a century than unaided faith as a means of healing has been able to do. It can be argued also that modern healing discovery was not possible until the religious reference of disease was put aside, until men disregarded religious ideas about disease and set about finding by their own work what really caused it and how the cause could be removed. However important a place faith may have in healing, and however great—and it is infinitely great—is the power of the message Christ brought, it remains clear that faith is not the only essential factor in healing. Modern science has proved this beyond doubt. It has been shown for ever that healing is not merely a religious business, and cannot just be kept in the hands of people who believe in a certain technique of faith and who regard the last word as having been spoken on the matter.

There is no doubt that modern experience testifies that great help can be given to neurotic people, and frightened patients, by the infusion of faith and trust. Indeed it is true to say that the hope of healing, with regard to any man, depends upon this element in him. On the other hand, the mere imitation of the New Testament pronouncements can be very harmful. Those who have worked among primitive peoples can testify that biblical and New Testament methods can be used by native believers which are utterly remote from any reality, and do harm. The mere telling of a disease to depart in the name of Christ or anybody else does not seem to be enough. It is necessary to know the causes of the disease and to make it depart by all the means in our power.

On the other hand, if faith is profoundly conceived, not merely as a magical means of producing healing, but as an attitude of the whole person, which unifies him and turns him towards the Ground of his being, which reconciles him with what is happening to him and takes away his fear, then here is something from which modern scientific healing can learn. As a matter of fact, modern healing seems prepared to do so. It has been long recognized that disease does not merely affect one part of a man. It affects the whole man, and very important in the healing is the unifying of the man, so that he can face what has happened to him, and so that he can derive strength in his situation. There are very few illnesses which do not put the whole man, as it were, at stake, and the attitude of the whole man and his unity and integrity in the experience are very important. The reference to the one God, and the certitude of His power to help, was the source of Jesus's power to help the demoniacs. These poor creatures, like the modern people who are in need of psychiatric help, were at war with themselves and out of their own control. The presence of One who referred the whole situation absolutely to God had a great tranquillizing effect. This was something more important than a medical procedure or trust in a doctor. It was an alteration of the whole situation by the realization that God was there to help.

FAITH IS NOT A TECHNIQUE: IT IS FUNDAMENTAL COMMITMENT

Thus faith is not a piece of technique to be imitated. Faith must be really there in the sense that it is operative to overcome the actual situation with all the means in its power. Faith is not just an acting in a set pattern; it is a facing of a situation. It can reveal itself in situations that are very far removed from the circumstances of the New Testament. For example, it can reveal itself in the researches of a man who is looking for a cure to a certain disease. He can only go on in the assumption that ultimately his researches, in spite of many failures, will be blessed; and without this faith his motive for working disappears.

Faith must be rescued from the faith-healers. It must be roundly stated that the setting up of a missionary hospital, with all the difficulties entailed, requires more real faith than that of the faith-healers; and the setting up of the hospital produces in its own ways more miracles, if by miracles we mean unexpected instances of the power and kindness of God, and the presence of healing in hopeless situations. There is no reason whatever why faith cannot be exemplified both in the discovery of scientific techniques and in the using of them. The attitude of the man who leads in these matters is of supreme importance and his trials in this work can only be sustained by faith in his mission and the value of his endeavour. It may not always be expressed in religious language, but fundamentally it touches the same reality. If faith means the setting of one's whole existence at stake in order to find or to prove something which brings health and release to mankind, then the discoverers of chloroform and radium show more faith than that of faith-healers, who are comparatively much less involved in what they are doing, and can say a great deal and seemingly do a great deal without much personal sacrifice. It is very easy for them to put the onus of faith on the patient and not on themselves. When such folk are compared with those who risked their lives to discover chloroform and who lost fingers in the pursuit of the qualities of radium, it is easy to see which of these people is most like our Lord Jesus Christ, who risked His all upon the Cross of Calvary.

At any rate Jesus was not deceived by words and the appearances of things. He was well aware that someone could look like Him and not be Him. In the parable of the two sons, one used the language of disobedience and the other that of obedience, but the former came to obey and the latter missed the whole meaning of the commandment. The faith-healer uses the language of the New Testament and takes up its posture of obedience, but it is often the scientific healer who overcomes circumstances by a real facing of them, and who shows by his devotion and suffering how much he cares for discoveries that can benefit mankind. Facing reality, with all the doubts and fears it produces, is often a far greater test of a man and his devotion and faith in his mission than the practice of a faith-healing that avoids the great problems which afflict mankind. Faith, if we mean by faith, not the blind acceptance of things on trust because they have the prestige of authority, but personal commitment and risk in order to act for the attainment of discovered truth or its application in some circumstance, is often as much a personal reality and necessity for the scientist in his devotion to science as for the religious man in his spiritual and ethical

THE SIGNIFICANCE OF THE N.T. HEALING MIRACLES 83

witness. The situations may be different, but the substance may be similar. Above all, this will apply to the Christian who is engaged in medical research or in the practice of scientific healing. There is no reason whatever why he should not exercise in his scientific calling the quality of faith which moves mountains.

THE NEW TESTAMENT IS NOT A SOURCE OF TECHNIQUE

The notion that some kind of healing technique can be extracted from the New Testament dies hard, and it is sometimes claimed that Jesus's approach to the sick provides a method of dealing with patients today, not merely in His compassion and understanding, but in the literal character of His words and actions. There are people who see our Saviour, in the healing miracles, adopting patterns of behaviour which are examples to be followed by healers in modern situations when they seek an entrance to people's needs. But let any pastor or psychiatrist try to conduct an interview with what he thinks is the most apposite story of Jesus's relation to a sick person in mind, and he will soon discover that he must have freedom. He will find what the New Testament emphasizes, namely, that we follow a risen Lord in the Spirit. The stories are vehicles of the Spirit, and not norms to be followed at all costs. What we find in the New Testament is not a technique, but the inspiration of a technique, the end and purpose of a technique, or the test of the value of a technique, not of its technical value but of its value as a spiritual thing in its effect upon humanity. The condemnation of the New Testament on what a man is doing, and the means that he is employing, is much more damning than a technical judgement.

THE RELIGIOUS REFERENCE OF DISEASE AND THE ATTITUDE OF JESUS

In the Old Testament health and sickness are looked upon as coming only from God. He alternates them at His pleasure. Sickness is a sign of God's wrath, and it cannot be removed until God forgives and restores. The Psalms are full of this realization. The Book of Job contains the struggle of the human spirit against it. It is clear that sickness and healing have a religious reference in the

Old Testament, and this dominates all thinking about them. This is the primitive notion of sickness general throughout the world, except that in the Old Testament it is monotheistically conditioned, while in the pagan world it is polytheistic. Sickness comes from the gods and thus we have special gods for particular illnesses —e.g. the cholera goddess of India and the smallpox god of Nigeria.

It is true that sickness affects the whole man and therefore puts him wrong with regard to the whole of existence; hence the feeling that he is under the wrath of God or the gods is natural enough. But while this may have on one side psychological value, on the other side it does tremendous psychological harm. The sufferer has not only the sickness to contend with, but also the God whose wrath sent it. The sickness thus becomes more difficult to deal with. Nevertheless it is a known fact that sickness often brings a feeling of guilt and that psychosomatic illnesses can be caused by such a feeling, and therefore should also be dealt with on that level. Still, progress in the advancement of knowledge and the control over human life have only come when the religious reference has been put out of mind, and observation and a factual appraisement have taken its place. But even on the religious level, the notion that all sickness stems simply from the wrath of God has proved to be a burden on the human spirit. True religion must contest this notion in order to preserve a proper relationship to God, and a realistic approach to the world.

Jesus lifts the whole matter of healing into another dimension. There is a sense in which He ignores the religious reference. He does not speculate about the origin of sickness in the wrath of God. In the Gospel of St John He specifically avoids doing so when questioned about the origin of a man's blindness (Jn 9[1]ff). He is primarily concerned, not with the origin of sickness, but with its overcoming. He thinks in terms of a straight fight between the Kingdom of Disease and the Kingdom of God. He is concerned above all with the God who gives new life. He has always the faith that every situation can be moved into freedom, that however closed it may appear to man, God can open it. This we have seen to be the essence and the basic truth of the notion of 'miracle'. Amid all the critical problems arising from the synoptic tradition, this is the one clear impression that remains. Jesus is not simply a doctor who adopts new methods. He seems to accept the rabbinic demonology of His time, and the physical aids He employs are of the most primitive—spittle and oil—nevertheless, He realizes the symbol of the healer in a manner which cannot be transcended.

THE CHARACTERISTICS OF JESUS'S ATTITUDE TO HEALING

(a) *Courage*

The first characteristic of the healing work of Jesus was a new courage. This feared neither the dark powers which control the human mind nor the religious institutions and sanctions which oppress it. If Jesus, as a man of His time, did not question the rabbinic demonology, He faced the demoniacs in the consciousness of a power that could control them. There was no passive acceptance of demon possession, as though it were a token of the wrath of God and nothing further could be done about it. The very regarding of sickness as to some extent a demonic force meant that it was seen as something extraneous to man and not an inevitable part of his lot. With His realization of the power of God breaking into human life, Jesus was able to create a new centre of consciousness, from which the dark powers could be objectively seen and dealt with.

This was what needed to be done in His situation, since scientific understanding did not then exist. No science was possible in a demon-haunted world. First, man had to free himself from fear of the dark powers. The world had to be cleansed before it could be objectively viewed, and it can perhaps be said that the growth of science in later centuries owed something to this cleansing.

Jesus also asserted fearlessly the right of the healer against religious sanctions and institutions. This was the meaning of the controversy raised in His time about healings on the Sabbath (Lk 6^6, etc.). Jesus thus established the right of the healer to proceed with his work whatever the religion of his time might be saying. Religious folk were shocked at His healing on the holy day, but for Him the patient was more important than the taboo, however august it might be. He was the Pioneer in a war which healing science has had to wage in many countries during recent centuries, not only in the East, where Karma was manifest in the diseases of men or doctors were refused admittance to the Zenanas for moral reasons, but also in the West, where religious folk objected to anaesthetics being given to women in difficult childbirth because of the Old Testament text which said that they should bring forth children in sorrow. The 'Christian Scientist' refuses on religious grounds to call the doctor, and the 'Jehovah's Witness' prevents the blood transfusion that would save his child. Religious taboo, horror of the unclean thing, masquerading as religious principle, has often tried to block the way to scientific healing, in research and practice, both in medicine and psychotherapy. Jesus put the sufferer first.

Though Jesus is working in an atmosphere remote from that of our modern civilization, His confidence that the dark powers which oppress mankind can be overcome and His refusal to allow any authority to prevent the work of healing are an inspiration to the modern healer. Jesus's courage in this matter is not merely a blind confidence that everything will give way at once for the man who feels he is doing God's work. He Himself is reported to have been a failure in Nazareth because of the lack of faith among the people to whom He was ministering, and we have records also of the disciples failing in their attempts to heal. Nevertheless, throughout the New Testament there is a consciousness that a new power has broken into the world in the life of our Lord Jesus Christ, to which everything must ultimately bow.

(b) *Depth*

Next to be noted is the depth of Jesus's notion of healing. It may be said that His conception embraces the whole man. It becomes a form of pastoral care. He is not like other healers, merely concerned with the bodily ailments which brought the man to Him. He sees the whole man in the whole situation. This explains His emphasis in some healings on the forgiveness of sins. It was not merely paralysis that was afflicting the paralytic. The trouble lay in deeper levels than the physical. Jesus worked to take away the sufferer's fear. While guilt is present all existence is feared.

Jesus accepted the whole man in his whole situation. This attitude of Jesus is reflected in that of the modern healer, who accepts the sufferer as he is, in his situation, without inquiring into the moral or spiritual failings which may have brought him into it. But to Jesus it was not merely a general acceptance of the man concerned. He worked to put the man right with the whole of his existence. Therefore He descended, as it were, into the depths of the man's spirit in order that he might be put right with God.

Jesus was aware of spiritual disturbances which affected the whole of a man's life. He saw the basic and initial error in a man, which had brought him to his present position. He put this right by the forgiveness of sins. Jesus was concerned also not to put a man right merely with himself and God, but also with society. He sent the cleansed lepers to the priests in order that they might enter into common life once again. The demoniac was clothed and sent home to his friends.

Although the foreground in the synoptic stories is taken up with wonderful healings, the background is concerned with a great reconciliation of man with his existence. The healing acts of Jesus are part of His great transference of the whole of life into a new dimension. He is concerned with the renewal of life through the Kingdom of God. Jesus brought into the world a very profound conception of healing. It concerned the whole man, body, mind and spirit; it concerned the whole of society, and the reconciliation of man with his existence. It was incomplete while any of these considerations was forgotten.

The growth of scientific healing has also been a development in the conception of the magnitude of healing. Today it does not merely treat man's bodily ailments; it takes into consideration man's inward or psychological condition, and is concerned with the whole man and where he stands with regard to his life and with regard to society. The willingness of Christian doctors and psychotherapists to refer patients in certain circumstances to ministers of the Word and Sacraments is a welcome acknowledgement that healing may be necessary at a depth beyond that of scientific method.

(c) Motive

The healings of Jesus have a new motive. We are in a new moral and spiritual atmosphere. The emphasis is simply on the life-giving, merciful God. The healing acts of Jesus spring from sheer mercy and love. They are a response to human need in the name of God and to human need without distinction.

In marked contrast to the Hellenistic stories of healing, there is no mention of payment in the New Testament. In the Greek stories the god who had done the healing at a particular shrine was very jealous that he should afterwards be paid, and brought punishment upon the man who tried to escape this responsibility. The motto of the New Testament is 'Freely ye have received, freely give' (Mt 10^8).

This, while it is the most obvious trait in New Testament healing, is also the most important. The inspiration for the modern healer lies just in this, that any power that is given to him to achieve healing is a power given by God and therefore should be used not for payment, not for prestige, not for the glorifying of any institution, but simply because God is a God who relieves suffering. The mercy which is revealed in the New Testament stories is the real life of the medical profession. When that is forgotten, the power often recedes from healing. Healing finds other motives and other aims. This is very apparent in countries where medical science has only recently penetrated. There is a big temptation on the part of men who have received European education in healing to use their power simply for their own advancement, and it often happens that the poor and the broken in primitive countries are no better for their own educated doctors, who are concerned to minister to those who can give them money for what they do.

It can be maintained, therefore, that Jesus, although He introduces no new methods of healing, can be said to be the symbol of all healing in that He reveals the courage which is prepared to face the existence of the sufferer in whatever condition he may be, without fear; in that He is concerned with a wide and deep conception of healing, which embraces the whole man in his whole situation; and in that the motive of the healing is sheer love of man within the revelation of the mercy of God.

THE MODERN HEALER AND THE CHRIST SYMBOL

Jesus's powers were regarded as miraculous by His contemporaries; we are controlled by other factors and think in scientific terms. Yet it is true to say that science has given man miraculous powers and the modern healer is in the position of being able to emulate the miracles of Christ. These wonderful new powers must be protected and controlled by His spirit.

If the scientific powers of healing were divorced from the basic courage to face what is in man and the world, divorced from a concern for the whole man and his whole condition within and without himself, and divorced also from considerations of mercy and love, from concern about people because they are precious to God, then scientific healing itself would degenerate, as it did in

Germany during Nazi persecution, into something utterly unworthy of man. Christ remains the symbol of the true healer, and the modern healer with his scientific power working in the spirit of Christ can again reincarnate and realize that symbol.

5
The Theology of Healing
William Strawson

THE THEOLOGY OF HEALING

THEOLOGY IS THE study of the nature and activity of God. The theology of healing deals with the nature of God as it is assumed and revealed in the practice of healing, and with the activity of God in the process of healing. But healing assumes disease; therefore the theology of healing must include a discussion of the nature and activity of God in relation to disease. And as disease is part of the 'problem of evil', this problem must be considered as well.

It will help to clarify our thinking if at the outset we say what a theology of healing is not, and what it cannot do. It is not a theodicy, either in the narrow sense of an attempt to justify the goodness of God in spite of the fact of evil, or in the wider sense of an attempt to explain the facts of disease and the technique of cure in terms of divine providence and human activity. If modern theology has learned one lesson from its recent past, it is that there are many problems to which there is no ready answer in Christian thought. Any suggestion that there can be a complete explanation of disease and its cure is recognized as foolish presumption. Whatever we can say about the nature and activity of God in relation to healing must never be taken as a claim to have explained all the mysteries and solved all the problems.

Again, it does not seem the proper task of a theology of healing to set out the conditions and methods by which men can bring spiritual healing to pass. It is necessary for men to study the facts of the spiritual realm as of the physical, but such a study does not properly belong to the theology of healing. Essentially this study concerns the nature and activity of God. The Christian theologian must think about the fact of disease and the fact of healing, and the theology of healing is the relating of these facts to the divine nature and activity.

The theology of healing we are to consider will be understood from a Christian point of view. While there are some elements in its view of healing which Christian theology holds in common with non-Christian faiths, the important factors in the Christian view are distinctive and unique. Because this has not been sufficiently realized, Christian theology is sometimes saddled with problems which arise out of non-Christian interpretations. A good example of this is the idea that resignation in the face of evil is the characteristic Christian reaction. But as Streeter shows, resignation is by no means the characteristic attitude to evil evidenced in the Gospels.[1] On the contrary, the attitude of our Lord was confidence in God, and recognition that evil was the work of Satan. This is not to say that there is no place in the Christian attitude for resignation, nor that the Christian cannot think of God as in any way responsible for disease, but these are not the chief or determinative aspects of the Christian view. The Christian view must be determined by the activity of Christ, as it is seen in the Gospels and the rest of the New Testament, and confirmed in Christian experience. This brings into prominence our Lord's healing miracles, and we must consider the principles underlying these miracles if we are to gain a satisfactory concept of spiritual healing from a Christian point of view.

The subject as thus outlined seems to fall naturally into two parts. There is the situation as it exists before healing takes place, the situation which presents a challenge to the faith and spiritual perception of those concerned in it. This is often a situation which presents great difficulty to the man of faith. Here we have to think of pain, disease, deformity, disability, weakness and death, all as existent realities. and we have to think of God in relation to these realities, for it is vain to suppose that the great resources of spiritual healing can be employed in a spiritual vacuum. It may seem attractive to argue that when some signal work of healing has been accomplished, faith in God is produced, but until such a thing takes place, the only possible attitude is scepticism. On the contrary, the man who cannot bring together his faith in God and the existent evil situation is not likely to apprehend enough spiritual truth to be able to find God at work in healing. This necessity of facing the problem of disease in the light of faith in God raises many questions, with which we must shortly deal. But we must not forget the second aspect of our subject. Not only have we to think of the situation as it is; we must also consider it as it ought to be and can be, in the light of our faith in God. This immediately raises the question of the inadequacy of resignation as the distinctive Christian attitude, for the Christian brings together his faith and the possibilities of the situation, and dares to believe that God will do something about it. This presents theology with the task of

[1] *Concerning Prayer*, p. 7.

attempting to describe the basis on which it can be asserted that God does use spiritual means to heal. This is especially a description of the ways God may be said to employ to effect healing, and is therefore more than the first part of the subject a discussion of divine activity, for the first part is mainly, but not exclusively, a discussion of existent facts and their relation to the love and power of God. But it is important to recognize that in both parts of the subject we shall be discussing both divine nature and divine activity, for these two must go together, and react upon each other. In other words, we shall be considering two questions simultaneously as we look at these two parts of the theology of healing. These questions are:

(1) What view of divine nature is asserted in this situation?
(2) What is God doing, and what is He willing to do, in the same situation?

In the first place we are to consider the facts of our human situation as they are affected by disease and suffering, and relate these facts to the God and Father of our Lord Jesus Christ. The facts seem so obviously opposed to the nature of God that it is a commonplace of religious thought that this is the most serious challenge to religious faith which is found in human experience. The problem of evil is one which has challenged Christian faith from the earliest days, both on an intellectual and experiential level. St Augustine was not the first to consider this problem, but his discussion of it is more thorough than most, and his famous work on the Freedom of the Will is mainly concerned with answering this problem. As Augustine shows, the difficulty affects the very basis of man's belief in God, and indeed the absence of a satisfactory answer to it has caused many to lose their faith altogether. Theologically the answer involves consideration of the freedom of the will and the meaning of the Fall, but Augustine is surely right in asserting that there is no explanation of the origin of evil in these traditional theories, although they do express truths about the fact of evil.

The same difficulty is felt by countless mortals when they face some suffering or tragedy. Why, if God is good and powerful, does He allow this evil thing to happen? It is true that sometimes this question has a selfish basis, but we shall be deceiving ourselves if we do not admit that it is often a question which arises out of deep perplexity, not least for the man of faith. The point of discussing it in this context is that unless we can have some satisfactory answer to the problem of suffering, we shall not be in a very good position to understand or use the divine resources which are available. It would be going too far to say that God cannot exercise His divine healing powers unless we have a satisfactory answer to the problem of evil, but at least we can say that if this problem causes us to stumble and to doubt either the goodness or the power of God, we are in a much less favourable position to co-operate in the divine work of healing. For we are not likely to enter into effective partnership with a God against whom we have a deep grudge or suspicion, or for whom we have positive hatred because of His apparent indifference to our suffering.

There are several ways of attempting to meet the difficulty posed by the fact of suffering in a world which is claimed to be the domain of an omnipotent and loving God. The least satisfactory approach is to try to maintain that suffering is not real. This is so blatant a contradiction of the facts of human experience that it would seem superfluous to mention it, were it not that a considerable body of people who are active in a type of spiritual healing make it their main assertion. It is therefore necessary to state without equivocation that it is no part of the orthodox position to deny the fact of suffering. We agree that mental attitudes do make a great difference to the intensity and length of suffering, for anticipation often adds to the reality of suffering, as does anxiety and apprehension about its cause and its development. But this is very different from saying that suffering is only in thinking, and the cure for it is to 'think positively'. A Christian should be a realist, and this means accepting the fact of suffering, which is not an illusion, and cannot be disposed of by ignoring it.

The next argument which is often used is that which claims that although suffering exists, it is not evil. Of the many forms of this idea the most popular is that which likens human life to the weaving of a piece of cloth. While the process is going on there seem to be many loose ends and the pattern is not discernible, but when the piece of cloth is finished and turned over, all is seen to be part of the pattern. Thus that which seems evil because it is unpleasant, and indeed painful, is really part of the divinely good plan which is being worked out. The same idea is put more intellectually by the assertion that evil does not exist *sub specie aeternitatis*. But, as F. R. Tennant argues, we have to live *sub specie temporis*, and here and now, evil is evil.[2] Even if it were an illusion it would still be an evil. There is of course specious support for the argument that suffering is good in disguise, in the fact that sometimes good does come out of suffering. But the fact that suffering is sometimes (not by any means always) productive of good, does not in any way validate the view that suffering itself is good.

A better argument, but still not conclusive, is that suffering is inevitable. There are two forms of this. On the one hand, it can be asserted with some plausibility that suffering is an inevitable part of the life of sentient beings, and as the most sensitive of all creatures, man is susceptible of the most intense pleasure and pain. The strength of this approach lies in its reference to man's mortal state. Man is a mortal creature, by nature having only a limited span of life. Something must intervene to terminate man's life, and this may well involve suffering. But it is not inevitable that it should do so, for in some cases, old age and death seem to be without pain or suffering of any kind, and there is apparently no reason why man should not live his mortal span in freedom from pain, and then at the end just cease to breathe. Again, the fact that suffering sometimes serves biological ends does not make it a necessary part of human existence, and we have to admit that much suffering seems to go far beyond any positive value either for the individual or the race.

The other form of the argument from inevitability takes a logical approach. It is said that the dilemma of the goodness of God and the reality of evil is based upon a logical contradiction. Particularly when the freedom of man is considered, it is said that for this freedom to be real, there must be the real possibility of the wrong choice. Out of this inevitable choice comes suffering for man, for man perversely chooses the bad instead of the good, and brings suffering on himself and on the race. Thus the fact of suffering cannot be directly the responsibility of God, for man has brought it upon himself by his choice of evil. This argument has often been advanced by Christian apologists, and there is some cogency in it. But, as Antony Flew has shown, the logical basis of it is not as sound as has often been supposed.[3] Flew argues that there is no logical contradiction involved in the possible creation of men who could only choose the good; this would not necessarily involve a denial of their freedom, since predictability and recognizable cause

[2] *Philosophical Theology*, II.181.
[3] *New Essays in Philosophical Theology*, pp. 144–69.

are not contradictory of freedom of choice. The value of Flew's discussion lies in the point that a Christian cannot explain the fact of evil as inevitable on the grounds of the necessity of freedom. There are also subsidiary arguments which tend in the same direction, such as that if all the suffering in the world is a necessary concomitant of man's moral progress as a free creature, the question arises whether the result is worth the cost. This then becomes an indictment of God's wisdom rather than His power and His love.

It is important to be clear what this argument involves. It does not prove that there is no such Being as the Christian describes as a good and omnipotent God; Flew himself wisely refrains from drawing this conclusion. All it means is that often Christians have tried to explain the fact of evil and suffering on erroneous assumptions. That is, the assumption that evil is a necessity is a false assumption. It may not be impossible to think about evil and God together, but the wrong way to do this is to suppose that evil is an unavoidable necessity. If at this point we add that it is not essential that the Christian faith should be able to provide an explanation for every event in the universe, we may be approaching a better understanding. Theology must not be content to remain under the logical veto, but it places itself in a very difficult position if it speaks of the inevitability of evil. Theology must here take the initiative, and from its own position make its own assertions about God and evil.

As we have said, the first assertion is that evil is a fact, and some suffering is part of the fact of evil. Christian thought does not properly claim to explain how evil came into existence, far less to explain that it is inevitable. Even the doctrine of the Fall does not really set out to give such an explanation, for if that doctrine is primarily an explanation of the origin of evil, it fails lamentably, since all it does is to push back the problem into the recesses of man's unknown original state of perfection. Many people have rejected the doctrine of the Fall because they have mistakenly supposed that it sets out to be an explanation of the origin of evil. But what the doctrine sets out before us is the fact of evil, and what it asserts is that this fact is not an individual phenomenon, but belonging to the whole race. Not only individual men do wrong acts, but also the whole human race is infected with evil, and evil has affected every part of human activity. From this we can assert that much of the suffering of man arises in his choice of evil, but this is not the same as saying that evil is necessary in order for man to have free choice.

The second assertion we can make is that God is actively opposed to evil in His world. Evil is that which opposes the good will of God, and is itself actively opposed by God. The whole story of revelation can be summed up by saying that it is the record of the divine opposition to evil. The Bible never tries to assert that evil does not exist, nor does it really attempt to say how it came into existence. The Bible is much more concerned with describing the action God takes to combat evil. This action includes the selection of Israel to be His own people, and culminates in the gift of God's own Son to be the final conqueror of evil. The whole of sacred history is the story of this dramatic struggle between God and evil, and from the experience of the Church we know that this struggle continues, although the supreme act by which evil will eventually be defeated has already taken place in the death and resurrection of Jesus Christ. It is in the light of this conviction that we can best evaluate the popular notion that God sends evil and suffering upon man as a punishment for sin. The Christian cannot believe that God deliberately 'sends' that which is opposed to His will. It may be that often there is a causal connection between sin and suffering, sometimes traceable to the person who undergoes the suffering. If also we take into account the vast ramifications of evil in the human race, we may well believe that most suffering is in some way connected with man's sin.[4] But what is a natural consequence must not be interpreted as a deliberate punishment sent by God. It may be that often we have to say that suffering just happens, and is part of the fabric of human life. But this does not mean that it is entirely separate from God and out of His control. 'God does not will everything that happens, but He wills something in everything that happens.'[5] Herein lies the basis for Christian hope, for there is no situation in which God is not present and at work, and His work is always directed to the destruction of evil and the upbuilding of good. In a later section we shall discuss the implications of this for the Christian view of healing, but here we need to note that even apart from healing of disease and relief of suffering, God's work is manifest in human suffering. For in suffering God teaches the importance of reliance upon Himself, and the transitoriness of human existence. It is

[4] Cf. B. H. Streeter, *Concerning Prayer*, p. 22.
[5] G. Aulen, *The Faith of the Christian Church*, p. 197.

no use the sceptic saying that these activities of God do not justify the tremendous weight of suffering which is borne by men, for in saying that good comes out of suffering, we are not saying that this justifies suffering, or provides a sufficient explanation of it. But the fact cannot well be denied, that there are some very important lessons we simply do not learn unless we pass through times of suffering. And not only are these lessons learned by those who bear suffering, but also the qualities of perseverance and sympathy are called forth from men by the fact of the suffering of others, as they are not by any other experience. All this, we repeat, is not an attempt to say that suffering is after all a good thing. It is an attempt to give content and meaning to the conviction that God is active in suffering, and that these are signs of His activity. Furthermore, it is not easy to overestimate the value of these divine activities; for the results they produce, such as care for other people, selfless devotion, fortitude and courage, are by no means of less value than perfect physical health, which is indeed a great blessing, but is not always accompanied by equal virtues and qualities.

It must never be supposed that the Christian makes these assertions about the activity of God in suffering lightly, or without thought for what suffering means for men. The Christian is not, after all, a mere spectator of human suffering, for he is part of suffering humanity, and must never suppose that his relation with God gives him a special immunity from the ills which afflict other men. This has to be said, because sometimes the sceptics give the impression that they alone know from personal experience what this problem of suffering really means. But the Christian knows it too, and this must save him from giving facile answers to these most trying problems. But even more, the Christian knows that, as he is not a spectator of human suffering, so neither is God Himself. Full justice cannot be done to the Christian view of the activity of God in suffering without reference to the Christian belief that in the Incarnation the Son of God took human nature upon Him, and this involved God Himself in the pains and sufferings of human life. The very fact of being made man necessarily involves the personal knowledge of human weakness and weariness. The possession of a human heart meant for Jesus the knowledge of human sympathy and grief; and supremely on the Cross, God Himself, the very Son of God, entered into the deepest possible experience of human suffering. This was not only physical pain, but also the anguish of seeing hopes dashed, confidence betrayed, and even the comfort of the divine presence apparently denied Him. It is no empty phrase when the Christian insists that whatever suffering man has to bear has been tasted by God Himself; and still in all the afflictions of His children, God is afflicted. It is this faith in the close fellowship with God in suffering that so many suffering people find the most significant experience in their life. It is indeed as great a task of Christians to see how God is related to suffering, as it is to discover how He is also related to healing. This is not just to provide an escape road in case our hopes of healing are not fulfilled, for it is a necessary conclusion of the whole Christian belief in the Incarnation, and the presence of God in all human life.

When we turn to consider the second part of our subject, namely the relation between God and healing, it is important to recognize that this is not to be thought of as an alternative to the discussion which has preceded it. In other words, we are not faced with the difficult choice of deciding between the alternatives of thinking about God either in connection with disease or in connection with healing. It is indeed essential that we think of the two aspects together, for unless we do we shall inevitably have a deficient view of one or the other. The God who heals is also the God upon whom we rely when there seems to be no healing, and we certainly must not believe in God only when healing is manifest.

In considering how we can think of God in relation to spiritual healing, it is obvious that we must be clear what is meant by the term 'spiritual healing'. There are two factors which appear to be involved. Firstly, the use of what are loosely termed 'non-physical' methods of healing physical defects. It is well to recognize that the dividing line between physical and non-physical methods of healing is often very vague, and many forms of accepted medical treatment manifestly use both factors in varying degrees. Indeed there may be no so-called physical methods of cure which do not draw upon some non-physical resources, and most non-physical methods involve some physical activity, such as laying on of hands or anointing. But even so, we accept the usual division of healing into those methods which predominantly use physical means and those which do not, and spiritual healing usually refers to the latter. But secondly, spiritual healing means the total healing of the human person—that is, not only his body, but his mind and his spirit. The ideal for this aspect of spiritual healing is a person completely integrated with his physical and spiritual environment. 'This complete health of the whole personality is what should be intended by the phrase "spiritual healing".'[6] It should be recognized immediately that such a definition of spiritual healing includes not only prayer and the anointing of the sick, but also surgery and psychiatric treatment, according to the nature of the illness which is being treated. A theology of healing must take into account not only those works of healing in which non-physical elements predominate, but also the more usual forms of healing, as practised by the medical profession. It may be that we shall only have clear ideas about the theology of healing in so far as we apply our views of divine activity to all aspects of healing—body, mind, and spirit.

But it is precisely when 'medical' and 'spiritual' methods of healing are contrasted that the difficulties begin to appear. Especially, medicine is seen to be a science, building up its knowledge by use of the scientific method of hypothesis, experiment, law; with results which are continually confirmed by pragmatic tests. Medicine involves training in careful diagnosis, and the application of medical and surgical treatment which by continual improvement is becoming more and more effective and reliable. Not all the problems facing medical science have been solved, and new problems in the form of hitherto unknown diseases continually arise. But the science of medicine has so far established and justified itself that with very few exceptions we go to the doctor when we have bodily ailments, and if he cannot bring us relief through the use of medical science, we generally accept the fact that our condition is for the present incurable. But in contrast to this, the common idea of spiritual healing is that it is unreliable, unpredictable, and mainly the province of cranks, who have no training, who do not accept the discipline of scientific method, and who make claims which cannot possibly be justified by the proper application of scientific method. Although this is a caricature of the more knowledgeable view of spiritual healing, it is not far from the attitude of many ordinary people, and not a few medical practitioners. There are of course many instances of supposed pragmatic proof of the methods of spiritual healing, which are fully accepted by the uncritical. But when these instances are subjected to careful scrutiny, we often find that the evidence falls short of proof. There is for one thing the great difficulty of diag-

[6] H. Anson, *Spiritual Healing*, p. 2.

nosis, for unless we can be sure beyond all doubt that a certain condition was present, we cannot claim that this condition has been cured. In very many cases where spiritual healing is claimed, the careful diagnosis is just not available. Again, it is necessary to follow up every case for a long period, in order to discover whether the supposed cure was permanent, or whether it was a temporary improvement due, for instance, to the excitement of a healing-service. In addition, it can be argued that even though the condition was as stated, and the cure appears to be permanent, it is possible that apart from the methods of spiritual healing, the ordinary processes of natural recovery would have operated, and therefore the supposed spiritual healing methods have in fact made no difference to the situation.

Yet when full allowance has been made for the excesses of some of the supporters of spiritual healing, it remains true that there is enough evidence to suggest that there is something in this approach, and there is increasing interest in non-physical methods of healing, both among the medical profession and in the Church. Although spiritual healing must not be equated with psychological methods of healing, the successes of psychiatric medicine have tended to reinforce the assertions of those who claim that spiritual methods can be effective. But a great gulf still exists between medical healing and the less generally accepted spiritual healing. One task of a theology of healing is to attempt to bridge this gulf. In attempting this we may also find that we have clarified our thoughts on the particular issue of spiritual healing.

To the Christian theologian this world is the sphere of divine activity. Without claiming that everything that happens is the direct and perfect will of God, we do assert that God is actively at work in the world. The idea that the relation between God and the world can be adequately expressed in terms of the celestial clockmaker, who has wound up the world and then left it to run on its own, is almost as remote from the Christian view as can be imagined. The Christian does not deny the reality of 'natural' powers, but he asserts that these powers derive their energies from God, and that through them God is actively at work in the world. This conviction applies equally to the normal functions of life, as well as to those occasions when special activity seems to be required in order to put right something that has gone wrong. In terms of our special interest, this means that the divine activity is just as much operative in the maintenance of health as it is in its restoration. When we are healthy, we are co-operating with the divine powers of health, and God is actively at work within us. Incidentally, it often takes a period of ill-health to convince us that this is so, for nothing is so easily taken for granted as good health. Thus when we are in need of medical attention, the doctor can only bring us restored health by helping us to co-operate with the divine forces of healing, which are expressions of divine activity. From this point of view the question of the validity of spiritual healing becomes clear. Those who affirm the reality of spiritual healing are saying that the divine activity of healing takes place through many channels. One of these channels is medical science, and this is never to be despised or avoided. But there are other channels, and the methods of prayer, anointing, laying on of hands, as signs of spiritual activities, are channels of divine activity. It is necessary to note that this in no way minimizes the importance of the doctor's training and skill. Many of the most impressive methods of healing have only been made available through the devotion of research workers, and the skill and patience of those doctors who have applied the results of research to particular problems of disease. All these varied activities of medical research and experiment are ways through which God pursues His healing work in the world. We have to conclude that God does not force knowledge upon men, but waits until men discover it. There are many challenges to medical science in our contemporary life, and the Christian must avoid giving the impression that he is only interested in those methods which do not use ordinary means at all. The work of research and of experimental methods of treatment is a work which is energized and inspired by divine grace.

What does this teach us about the particular place of religion in healing? For one thing, we are encouraged to see that the secret of any effective healing is co-operation with the divine forces of healing. This means that it is a tremendous help if the patient who is being treated for any malady whatsoever has the attitude of faith and confidence in God which opens his life to the divine powers of healing. This is not merely giving a religious twist to the well-known fact that without confidence in the physician the patient will not receive full benefit from any treatment. It is rather that, since the doctor is doing a divine work, whether he admits it or not, the patient can do a great deal to make that work effective by his own attitude to God. If the patient is insensible to the work of divine grace, even more if he is resentful of his illness, he may be blocking one of the ways used by God to effect the healing of his body. Again, this co-operation with the divine healing powers is not limited to those who are being treated, but also includes those who pray for the person affected. It is impossible for us to give a complete explanation of how prayer can make any difference. There is sufficient evidence that it does so for the claim to be made that, without understanding the mechanisms involved, the Christian has every reason for using this means of co-operating with the divine resources. We shall return to this subject in our subsequent discussion of intercession, but for the moment we are concerned to show that this aspect of healing applies in all methods of healing, and is not to be limited to those occasions when little or no help can be obtained from medical science. Prayer is not a substitute for medical skill, but is needed alongside the proper employment of that skill.

Although there is ample scope for the concept of spiritual factors in healing even in methods which employ predominately physical means, the greatest problems and opportunities for Christian theology arise when non-physical methods of healing are considered. If we take as a specimen case the patient whose condition is such that medical science has admitted defeat, what are the issues raised for theology in the practice of spiritual healing?

The first difficulty which will occur to many is that we appear to be expecting God to break His own laws. If all the known resources of medical science cannot find an answer to this condition, are we supposing that because of our importunity God will alter the laws governing this disease, and allow a cure? But to think in this way is surely to misunderstand the position both of medical science and of spiritual resources. When medical science provides an answer to a situation of illness, it does not follow that this is the only answer; indeed, medical science is continually finding better methods of treatment. Similarly, when medicine says it cannot cure, it goes quite beyond its proper province if it goes on to say that there is no cure. If, then, through spiritual means a cure is effected, this is only a further instance of the same healing power which might have been used through medicine if only the right method had been known. When God heals through prayer, there is no more a breaking of divine laws than when He heals through more regular means. Some Christians assert that spiritual healing is the employment of higher laws which are at present unknown, or at least inexplicable in terms of known laws. This is an attractive idea, which seems a good answer to charges that prayer is based upon the assumption that God will break His own laws. But the concept of a 'higher, unknown law' is a difficult one in the philosophy of religion, since 'law' is here being used in a confusing sense. A law of nature is a description of the way in which events have been observed to happen. One assumption of the concept is that there is consistency in the universe to such a degree as to make it reasonable to say, on the basis of many instances, that events will continue to occur in the same way as they have so far been observed. The law is a statement of observed happenings, of how events have taken place, not of how they must proceed. In view of this, it will be seen that the concept of an unknown, higher law is really a misnomer, for there can be no observation of the unknown. It is also somewhat confusing to call this a higher law, as if in some sense it is superior to known laws. In so far as the laws of nature are descriptions of how natural events take place, there can be no higher or lower law. One set of events may indeed appear to contradict the observed laws relating to another set of events, but when this occurs a new law has to be formulated to describe the observed facts. This new law is not a higher law, except in the sense of being more comprehensive. No doubt those who use this expression are seeking to assert that the events which seem to be outside the known laws of nature are nevertheless not haphazard happenings, but are consistent with the total nature of things. This is a proper conviction, but it is misleading to use the term 'unknown law' in expressing it.

A problem related to this is put in the form of the question: 'Do miracles still happen?' When some striking instance of healing has taken place it seems natural to refer to it as a miracle, but like the term unknown law, miracle is a misleading expression to use in this connection. If we say any unexplained event is a miracle, we have to admit that many events which were formerly inexplicable are now open to explanation. This means that in terms of the definition of miracle as the unexplained, they have ceased to be miracles. Thus miracle becomes a temporary expression, applied to an event only so long as no explanation is available. The progress of human knowledge therefore is at the same time a continual reduction of the miraculous. The effect of this on the structure of the Christian faith could be very serious, for it could mean that eventually all the so-called miracles of Jesus would be explicable in terms of known phenomena, and the miraculous element in the Gospel story would cease to have any significance. Already indeed there are signs of this happening, especially in connection with the healing miracles of our Lord, some of which are now explained as having been brought about by psychological and other methods which are well known to us. The result is that Jesus seems to be remarkable only in that He knew the right psychological methods to employ long before modern psychology had been invented. Without being obscurantist, we have to admit that this attitude considerably reduces the stature of our Lord, and grievously misinterprets the meaning of the Gospel miracles. For these are presented in our records as signs of His divine powers, as acted parables which draw attention to His divine nature. In their setting in the Gospels, the miracle stories preach Christ as the Son of God and the Saviour of the world. If we give all our attention to the methods described in the working of miracles we may well be concentrating on the wrong issues, for these details are recognizable traits of all miracle stories, and may indeed be invented to make the story memorable and convincing. But to the Gospel writers the important fact was the work which Jesus performed, for this revealed His majestic rule over evil powers, and His divine origin and relation to God the Father.

If then this view of miracle as an unexplained happening is inadequate, we must look for a better one. A much more satisfactory view is that a miracle is a divine act outside the realm of ordinary events, by which God works His saving will for His children. Supremely this divine act is seen in the Incarnation of the Son of God, and it is better for us to try to understand miracles in general from this point of view than to try to arrive at a general definition of miracle and then apply it to the miracles of the gospels. The miracles of Jesus are *sui generis*, determinative and definitive. As they are the signal acts of divine salvation, they can never be repeated or explained. Our proper attitude to them is not attempted repetition, but adoring love and lowly reverence. They are so different in nature from all other events that it is better to limit the term miracle to these events in the life of our Lord, and express in other words our conviction that the work of God still continues in the world. This would suggest that the proper answer to the question 'Do miracles still happen?' is that the mighty works of God still continue, but these are through events which man's knowledge increasingly understands. The miracles of Jesus on the other hand, being manifestations of the Incarnation, can never be fully understood or explained. This view is more satisfactory than the idea that miracles still happen, on two counts. Firstly, it safeguards the uniqueness of the mighty works of Jesus, and frees us from the need to explain them in terms of other known experiences. Secondly, it avoids the easy credulity which regards any unexpected or unusual happening as a miracle. When such events are subsequently explained as natural events, or discounted because of evidence, the concept of miracle receives a serious setback. It is necessary to emphasize that this view in no way denies the reality of divine activity, both in maintaining the universe, and in healing disease and preventing disasters of all sorts. God does work in His world. We have no need to say that all His work is miraculous, unless we are prepared to evacuate the term of all true meaning. God is at work in the growth of every flower, in the development of every human person, in natural phenomena of all sorts. Some of these processes are partly explicable; others remain for the present a mystery beyond our comprehension. But they do not cease to be works of God when they are partly or even fully explained. It is better therefore to use the word miracle of those acts which were manifest in the life of Jesus, which demonstrate His divine nature, and which also indicate the purposes and concern which govern the divine activity in the world.

A more subtle danger facing those who believe in the effectiveness of spiritual healing is that they may appear to be depending on the notion of a special providence. This means that those who pray for themselves or their loved ones seem to suppose that they come under a different rule of providence from that which controls the lives of all other men. Sometimes it seems as if Christians, by their belief in prayer and divine intervention, aim at contracting out of the world and the sorrows and afflictions which fall upon the human race. The problem is seen in its severe form when a hospital ward is considered in which there are several patients suffering from the same illness. One of them, being a member of a Church, is visited by the minister, and prayed for by the congregation. He recovers, but the others die. What conception of God is involved in this situation? Should the Christian expect to recover if the other patients in the ward do not? It is of course a wholly unworthy answer to the problem to say that the others could have been members of Churches, and received the benefit of pastoral care and Christian fellowship if they had thought of God when they were well. True as this is, it does not really meet the situation. There are better things we can say, even if they do not supply all the answers to this very common problem.

The difficulty is eased, if not completely met, by the fact that when a minister visits such a ward to pray with his member, he usually includes all the others in his petitions. The presence of the Christian brings more intercession into the ward, for the benefit of all. When the other patients see one of their number being cared for in this way, they may be led to pray for themselves, and for one another. This is especially the responsibility of the Christian, if he is able, for he should encourage the atmosphere in which men pray for themselves and for each other.

Perhaps the best approach to this question is a reminder that all healing is of a particular and personal nature. Operations are not performed *en masse*; medicines are not laid on by pipe line to every bed in the ward indiscriminately. Every illness has to be treated individually, however much it conforms to a general pattern. In the same way, the powers which come through prayer come to the person for whom prayers are said, not equally to everyone. This is one of the given factors of human existence, and there is no more unfairness involved in some being prayed for while others are not, than there is in some receiving the right medical treatment while others do not. But it may be objected that in the former situation God alone is responsible, and in the latter situation man prevents equal treatment from being available to all, through political and economic factors and so on. But this objection is not valid, since all divine healing, of whatever kind, comes through human co-operation. It may be no more surprising for one patient to recover who has the benefit of proper spiritual care, than it is for another to do so who has proper medical care. In both cases God uses human agency, and if it is lacking in either of them, God cannot be blamed if healing does not take place. So the man who is prayed for is not expecting to be treated by God in a special way not available to others. He is drawing upon divine resources of healing which he believes are also available to others, and which are effective only in the right conditions of human response and spiritual awareness.

This conclusion lays a great responsibility upon the Church, which has the responsibility of interceding for all men. It is fairly common for the point to be made that many patients in hospital are never visited, and this is a proper call upon the charity of

Christian men. But how much more is it the responsibility of the Church that so many sick people are never prayed for! Here lies one of the greatest tasks of the Church, for if we really believe that prayer makes a difference we shall wish all men to have the benefit of it. This makes much feverish activity in our churches appear just a stupid waste of time compared with our duty of intercession on behalf of the sick.

Most of the issues we have discussed come to a focal point in the question: 'Can prayer really make any difference?' This has always been a problem to the man who tries to live in a real world of cause and effect, which appears to be governed by reliable laws, and in which it is therefore difficult to see a place for prayer. Many conclude that prayer derives its effectiveness from the good it does to the one who prays, not to the person who is prayed for. A modern religious philosopher puts it in this way: 'It would be inhuman to forbid a mother to pray for her sick child, or even to forbid men to pray for themselves or others in time of danger. Yet must not such prayers be regarded as the satisfaction of a human need rather than a means to instruct or influence the divine will?'[7] But this difficulty is met if it is recognized that while science can properly describe and partly explain what does happen in the natural world, it cannot say what can or cannot happen. No doubt it is true that some belief in prayer is quite unreasonable, especially when prayer is regarded as a substitute for human action. But the Christian refuses to believe that he can do good only to himself by his prayers. Indeed when this limited view of the efficacy of prayer is accepted, it soon ceases to have any significance at all, and man ceases to pray. As we have said before, we cannot hope to produce a rationale of how prayer works. We do not pray because we have a complete explanation of the mechanism of prayer but because we are convinced that God welcomes our requests; and we have the example of our Lord, reinforced by many words of scripture, to compel us to regard prayer as the most natural act in the world. When he prays, the Christian is not expecting God to alter His plans for the future; he is bringing to God the factor of his interest and obedience, in the conviction that these will contribute to the way events will develop in the future.

Mention has been made in this essay of the need for more thought about the training and discipline needed in spiritual healing. This is evident when the question of prayer is considered.

[7] H. J. Paton, *The Modern Predicament*, pp. 356–7.

THE THEOLOGY OF HEALING 109

There is a danger that by emphasizing techniques we may give the impression that effective prayer is dependent on knowing the right technique, and on nothing else. But while we can learn a great deal about methods of prayer, we must never suppose that God only hears prayer that is offered in 'the right way'. Prayer is so much an intimate relation between man and God, that we have to admit that if anyone comes to God, however haltingly or fearfully, he will be answered according to the great love of God, not according to the excellence of his technique. Common Christian experience suggests that prayer should be both private and corporate, the one helping the other; it should be the expression of confidence rather than doubt; it should be constant; and it should be believing. That is, while it is sometimes necessary to agonize in prayer, more often all that is required is the simple prayer, said in faith, leaving the issue to God. Even intercession should not be only asking for things, but listening to the voice of God and being willing to obey it. Such prayer never goes unanswered, although the particular request which prompted the prayer may not be granted. The problem of unanswered prayer is one which ceases to have great significance when Christian prayer is offered in faith. This is not because the Christian always gets all he prays for, but because in his prayers he finds a deeper understanding of the will of God. This does not provide a complete answer to every problem, and often the Christian has to continue long in prayer, until an answer is given. But the opportunity for prayer is also an opportunity for growing in the knowledge of God, and in the power to continue in prayer, or the realization that the particular object of prayer is no longer to be requested. One of the most valuable by-products of intercession is a growing sensitiveness to the needs of others, and to the direction which is being taken by divine grace. As prayer is the willing co-operation of man with God, there seems no reason to suppose that very long prayers are necessarily more effective than short ones. When prayer becomes a vigil, lasting all night and even longer, one is bound to ask whether this type of exercise is intended to persuade God to do something which otherwise He would not do, or whether it is mainly a way of demonstrating devotion in the hope of generating greater concern for the project which is being prayed about. Again, while no doubt there is advantage in many people praying for the same object, we must never suppose that the effectiveness of intercession is in direct relation to the numbers involved. To extend the circle too widely is to lose the necessary interest and contact which is required for effective, believing prayer. Yet it is true that the more people there are who are praying, the more there are who are making their contribution to the divine purposes. A further point is that there is a limit to the range of anyone's effective prayer, and it is better to pray for a few objectives in an intelligent and interested way, than it is to pray perfunctorily for a large number of things.

The greatest contribution theology can make to the understanding of spiritual healing is to give it scope and direction. Too often we look upon the work of healing as confined to the restoration of this present limited and mortal state. But if we look at the matter from the fully theological point of view, we shall discover two great truths. Firstly, the objective of spiritual healing is wholeness—of body, mind, and spirit. These are but aspects of the human personality, which is not truly itself unless it is totally integrated and fully operative in all its aspects. The scope of spiritual healing is therefore true soundness of the whole personality. This soundness ideally means complete bodily, mental, and spiritual health. But as we live in a world which is affected by sin, we have to recognize that the ideal is rarely realized, and even when it is, it does not last very long. We are inclined to think that the chief aspect of this wholeness is bodily health. This is certainly the most noticeable aspect, but that is not to say it is the most important. Indeed there can be a closer approximation to the ideal of complete soundness in a body which has defects but which is occupied by a spirit in tune with God, than in a perfect body which is the home of a spirit which is deformed because it is out of relation with God. It is possible for man to be so interested in his physical welfare that he forgets his spiritual needs. This is revealed in the self-pity and self-centredness which can so easily mar the best desires for healing. In many cases those who think their greatest need is for physical health are most in need of deliverance from those defects of the soul which appear as self-centred pity. We shall never understand the depth of divine power until we realize that God sees our greatest need, and this is often not what we or others think it is. Some approaches to spiritual healing reveal a failure to grasp this most important fact. In all uses of spiritual healing there is need to remember that while man's body is important and is God's concern, the most significant part of man is that element through which he can have fellowship with God. The Church fails if those who come for physical healing are not made aware of their greater need of reconciliation with God through Christ. This reconciliation is not just a poor consolation for those who do not receive physical health; it is the vital factor in their healing, without which health of body may be a very inadequate and temporary benefit. The other contribution which theology can make to the understanding of spiritual healing is to set out the purpose of the divine activity which is evident in the healing process. This process is but part of the great renewing and developing power which is at work in the world. The object of this divine activity is to develop and perfect the creation of which man is part. To say that there is a divine purpose at work in the world is to imply that this world is evolving from what it is now, to some greater thing that it will be in the future. We are accustomed to think of the natural world as the result of the process of evolution, and as still involved in that process. As Pierre Teilhard de Chardin has so powerfully expressed in his *The Phenomenon of Man* and *Le Milieu Divin*, the future prospect is of man's spiritual development to a height that will far outstrip his physical growth. The means for accomplishing this, which is the same as that which sustains the process of evolution, is the divine power which provides both the environment and the objective of spiritual growth. In this context spiritual healing not only repairs defects in man's physical and spiritual nature, but also provides for greater growth and development. The powers of God which are available to man are such as can continue man's development far beyond its present stage. This means that through prayer and spiritual understanding we are able to release into the world vast reserves of power, which alone can complete the creation in the way God intends. But if such a power is accessible to us, how much more likely is it that there is sufficient power to overcome the present temporary ills and weaknesses of human nature.

Spiritual healing, therefore, must be based upon confidence in the power as well as the love of God. The way forward is through devotion to God in all our activities, not only so that we may receive healing, but so that we may develop more fully those spiritual capacities through which all the divine resources will be available to us. In this sense spiritual healing is not a special interest of a few Christians, for it is intimately related to the whole spiritual life of individuals and communities. As we learn what God is doing for our physical needs, we may also begin to learn more of the wonderful spiritual treasures which are ours in Christ.

6

Prayer and Healing

Ronald V. Spivey

PRAYER AND HEALING

IN THE APSE at Wesley's Chapel there is a stained-glass window portraying St Peter healing the impotent man at the Gate called Beautiful. The window, presented in 1891 on the occasion of the centenary of the death of John Wesley, was the gift of the Primitive Methodist Conference, and the legend says it was a witness 'of our essential unity in Methodism'. It is interesting that the Primitive Methodists should choose this particular incident to portray their emphasis in the essential unity of Methodism, for I believe the account of this incident in the Acts of the Apostles contains one or two of their favourite texts for the powerfully evangelical sermons they certainly preached. The words of St Peter on that Pentecostal occasion were the keynote of their evangelistic zeal: 'Silver and gold have I none, but whatsoever I have I give thee: in the name of Jesus of Nazareth, walk.' Certainly these early preachers had no silver and gold to give away, but in proclaiming the Gospel they shared a treasure of great price. The unsearchable riches of the Christian Gospel were summed up in that other great and popular evangelical text which concludes and underlines the meaning of the same incident of the healing of the impotent man, namely: 'In none other is there any salvation; neither is there any other name under heaven that is given among men wherein we must be saved.'

I must confess that although I was brought up with the 'evangelical' ring of that text echoing in my ears, it has only been quite recently that I have realized the importance of the fact that the whole point of the story is not that the man became a good Primitive Methodist but that he was enabled to walk! How many of us equate these great evangelical texts about the salvation Jesus offers with moral and spiritual blessings only? None of the four commentaries on the Acts of the Apostles which I possess so much as mentions the connection between the meaning of the word 'salvation' and the fact that the impotent man walked again. Yet this fact it was which caused St Peter to proclaim:

If we this day are examined concerning a good deed done to an impotent man, by what means this man is made whole; be it known unto you all, and to all the people of Israel, that in the name of Jesus Christ of Nazareth, whom ye crucified, whom God raised from the dead, even in him doth this man stand here before you whole. He is the stone which was set at nought of you by the builders, which was made the head of the corner. And in none other is there salvation: for neither is there any other name under heaven, that is given among men, wherein we must be saved (Acts 4^{9-12}).

In his *Notes on the New Testament* John Wesley says of this passage: 'The apostle uses a beautiful gradation from the temporal deliverance which had been wrought for the poor cripple, by the power of Christ, to that of a much nobler and more important kind, which is wrought by Christ for impotent and sinful souls. He therein follows the admirable custom of his great Lord and Master, who constantly took occasion from earthly to speak of spiritual things.' True though this may be so far as it goes, we must beware of the error of regarding all the miracles of Jesus as parables of 'spiritual' things. While, indeed, the miracles may illumine truth, they were neither parables nor sermon illustrations but actual events in which the word of salvation was made flesh and dwelt among men.

It is important to realize that in the Gospels the word translated 'salvation' refers to a wholeness of life in which physical and spiritual things are not separated as they are in the quotation from John Wesley's *Notes*. Indeed, in the first English translation of the New Testament John Wyclif consistently translated this word (*soteria*) as 'health', with some very interesting results, such as these:

In Luke 19^9 Jesus says to Zaccheus, 'This day is health come to thy house';
In Luke 1^{77}, in the Benedictus, 'To give the science of health to His people by the remission of their sins';
In Romans 1^{16} St Paul is not ashamed of the gospel because it is 'the virtue of health for believers'; and
He also exhorts the Philippians to 'work out your own health in fear and trembling for it is God that worketh in you.'

To us, who are so used to the unbiblical division between the 'physical' and the 'spiritual', Wyclif seems to be very unevangelical, but we must remember that he regarded 'health' as a state of life in which the physical and the spiritual man were united in loving response to God.

The translators of the Authorized Version of the scriptures did not follow Wyclif's translation, but, unfortunately, translated the Greek verb (*sozo*) in two ways—as 'save' when the translators considered the connotation was not primarily physical, and as 'make whole' when they considered it was. This is unfortunate for us, because it has made us think that health and personality and a right relationship with God are separable into 'physical' and 'spiritual' aspects, whereas they are not—and this is one of the discoveries which modern science is making. It is interesting, and not without significance, that in our English language the words 'wholeness' and 'holiness' come from the same root, so that the phrase 'wholeness of life' may well be the best rendering of what is meant by both 'health' and 'salvation'.

The fact that in the Bible view of man there is no real division between body and soul, and that these words represent different aspects of the same unit of personality, is most important, because it means that the words 'health' and 'salvation' are but different aspects of human wellbeing. Body and soul are not separate in such a way that one can properly be understood except in its relationship to the other. A doctor has to deal not only with diseases and a minister has to deal not only with sins; both have to deal with people and to cure them whether their vocation is a cure of souls or of bodies, and these fields inevitably overlap.

The denial of this truth has been responsible for that very materialistic outlook which has caused many medical men and women to think of disease as a breakdown of a purely physical mechanism. Tennessee Williams has expounded this view of life in his play *Cat on a Hot Tin Roof*:

When you are gone from here, boy, you are long gone and nowhere. The human machine is not so different from the animal machine, or the fish machine. It is just a whole God damn lot more complicated and more trouble to keep together.

With such a belief about human nature Niagaras of medicine and months of analysis leave a patient little better. Yet it is interesting to speculate why Mr Williams found it necessary to introduce two theological terms, albeit only as livid adjectives, into his description of the human machine! Did he find this oath necessary to counteract an otherwise bald and unconvincing description of human nature? This barren materialistic view of life has never satisfied men for long, and our own time is not the first in which the prevalence of this view in orthodox medicine has resulted in the rise of many religious sects claiming special powers of healing and not at all embarrassed by the charge that their thought and practice are irrational and unscientific. Indeed, religion itself has sometimes become so sufficiently unbiblical as to seek to make capital out of this erroneous dichotomy between body and soul by claiming that only the 'spiritual' matters. Even today this can lead to an emotional evangelicalism which so 'spiritualizes' the meaning of salvation that it becomes little more than an emotional experience and has no longer any vital connection with good news for the whole man.

Yet if, on the one hand, experience has shown that a materialistic view of human nature is an impediment to the cure of disease, the Bible, on the other hand, gives no ground for limiting the Gospel of our Lord Jesus Christ to the enjoyment of 'spiritual' experiences. Happily there are signs both in medical and pastoral thought and practice that this division of man into two separate compartments of 'soul' and 'body' is no longer acceptable or workable. May it even be that the rift between scientific and religious thought may begin to be healed as both combine in the treatment of suffering? Should this be so I believe it will be to the great advantage of scientific and religious thought alike.

'Health' and 'salvation' both describe the whole man at his best, and dis-ease is that lack of integration which works against his wholeness. The doctor and the minister are both the servants of God to this end, yet many scientifically-trained people are nervous of the intrusion into the field of health of those who believe in what they call 'spiritual healing'. I believe this nervousness to be justified, because there are very many healing sects whose belief and practice are not founded on the essential unity of body and soul which I have affirmed. Personally I do not use the phrase 'spiritual healing', because it might suggest some type or method of healing which does not consider physical symptoms or methods. If I have to use an adjective I use the phrase 'divine healing', because at least it indicates my conviction that all healing comes from God, whether He uses prayer or penicillin or psychiatry or plastic surgery as His method for restoring wholeness to our lives.

I believe it is most important to avoid the phrase 'faith-healing', because such a phrase throws the onus of responsibility on the believer, and while faith is indeed necessary to health as to salvation, the power which heals and saves is the grace of God. The word of St Paul is relevant here, though I do not think he was thinking primarily of physical wellbeing when he wrote to the Ephesians: 'We are saved by grace, through faith.'

Similarly we should avoid talking about 'healers'. There may be, and I believe there are, those among us who have a special 'gift' through touch or some other method whereby they can bring relief and mediate healing to sufferers. I believe this, also, to be a gift of God, and therefore not to be considered in opposition to or superior to other methods of healing.

In seeking to foster the development of the Christian ministry of healing along the lines of this thesis, the Church is not disowning the approach of orthodox medical practice, but rather offering help at a point of frustration.

In *The Spectator* of 30th November 1956 there was an interesting article entitled 'The Coming Crisis in Medicine'. In it the writer expounded the need for a far more searching and systematic attack on the basic causes of ill-health. He said: 'Diseases are not so much entities in themselves as the products of the interaction between the human constitution and the stresses to which it is exposed', and he emphasized the importance of the *stresses* and *interaction* to explain his contention that 'by far the greatest medical problem of the present day is to achieve understanding of the working of the mind'.

From a very different source comes the following description of a visit Professor Paul Tillich paid to Central Europe:

What I saw was a sick people, sick as a whole and sick as individuals. Their faces are shaped by burdens too heavy to be carried, by sorrows too deep to be forgotten. And what their faces expressed their words confirmed: Tales of horror, stories of pain and despair, anxieties dwelling in their blood, confusions and self-contradictions disturbing to their minds . . . old hostilities are smouldering, new hostilities are growing, and there is no peace. A sick nation.

But within this nation I found a people who were healthy, not because their sickness was not written in their faces also. But something else was in them, a healing power, making them whole in spite of their disruption, making them serene in spite of their sorrow, making them examples for us all of what could and should happen to us.

In view of this picture which we all recognize as true of much of our modern world and its need, are not Christians bound to consider how their faith can be related to the very material needs of mankind today? Consider this most challenging word of our Lord's about the relation between faith and material problems:

Verily I say unto you, Whosoever shall say unto this mountain, Be thou taken up and cast into the sea; and shall not doubt in his heart, but shall believe that what he saith cometh to pass; he shall have it. Therefore I say unto you, All things whatsoever ye pray and ask for, believe that ye have received them, and ye shall have them (Mk 11$^{28-4}$).

There would seem to be little room for doubt that when Jesus said this, He was speaking figuratively and using intentional exaggeration in order to impress His hearers with the importance of faith. Yet even when we have made all allowances for Eastern hyperboles, few people believe in the power of faith in any way which this text could be used to describe. Rather than accept the words of Jesus at anything like their face value we would prefer the way of Mahomet who moved to the mountain because the mountain would not move to him! We do not really believe that mountains can be moved, because, since they are mountains and part of this material universe, we believe that they will always keep their place unless man undertakes a complicated engineering enterprise or invents a nuclear mountain remover. We admit that human ingenuity expressed in engineering or the discovery of nuclear energy might succeed in removing mountains, but that is very different from faith. So we frequently end our exposition of this text by flatly contradicting what Jesus says. Mountains are mountains, we hold, and ought to stay in their place. Is what Jesus meant so absurd, therefore, as to be irrelevant?

Some time ago I heard a lecture on 'Science and the Christian Faith', given by a research physicist, which made me begin to realize that perhaps this text is not so utterly unrealistic and unscientific as I once thought, because instead of talking about the irrelevance of faith, the lecturer seemed to be questioning the immovability of mountains. I had been brought up to accept the 'laws of nature' as fixed and immovable, and like most of my generation had accepted the quotation from William Wordsworth which used to be the motto of the periodical *Nature*, as the necessary and adequate expression of the modern world view, namely: 'To the solid ground of nature trusts the mind that builds for aye.' The mountainous solidity of nature seemed secure. I had been taught that matter was made up of atoms and molecules which were as solid as billiard balls, and experience had taught me that billiard balls are very solid and only go where they are pushed! The world picture I had inherited from school was one which was based on unbreakable laws, the absolute solidity of matter, and the ability to measure all things in time and space.

Admittedly I went to school some years ago and my knowledge of physics has not kept pace with my use of radio and television. So when I heard a physicist talking about a really up-to-date world view I found it was very different from the one I had been taught. He affirmed that matter is not solid as I used to think of it, that the theory of relativity has done away with any absolute measurement in time and space, and that even what is seen—I quote his own amazing words—'depends on the perceiver as much as on the thing perceived'. What has happened to the immovable mountain? It is still there, of course, but it is no longer solid in the way I used to think; its greatness is only relative, and in some strange way it is only a mountain because I think it is! Wordsworth's 'solid ground of nature' has become such a less secure trust for 'the mind that builds for aye', that the editor of *Nature* has appropriately dropped the quotation from the front page! The 'eternal laws of nature' have ceased to be eternal, and the older scientific view on which we over-fifties were brought up seems to have suffered a sea change into something more like Prospero's island which was full of strange noises, and

> *These our actors*
> *As I foretold you, were all spirits, and*
> *Are melted into air, into thin air;*
> *And, like the baseless fabric of this vision,*
> *The cloud-capped towers, the gorgeous palaces,*
> *The solemn temples, the great globe itself,*
> *Yea, all which it inherit, shall dissolve,*
> *And, like this insubstantial pageant faded,*
> *Leave not a wrack behind.*

I do not mean that my lecturer said that the world was unreal; but he certainly said that my way of thinking about reality was out of date. The mountain is not quite so impervious or solid as I used to think. Indeed, it may well not require what I used to call a miracle to remove it. The newer world view of physics requires a newer theological view of what we mean by miracle.

The argument about miracles which used to occupy so much of the debate between science and religion, and is still heard in matters of healing, seems now to require a different approach. So long as the scientific world view was one in which even the smallest particles of the material structure of the universe had to follow a prescribed and invariable course, prayer seemed irrelevant and miracle an interruption of the natural order. It was difficult to conceive of any way in which God could break this natural sequence of events which He had created. Personally I found even the ingenious way over the difficulty propounded by St Thomas Aquinas somewhat unconvincing. This Thomist view may be summarized by saying that God is explained as the First Cause of all things, including all the secondary causes which He ordained. Because He is Sovereign Lord of all creation, He could interfere actively in the world process by suspending the course of natural events while an intervention was made and then by restoring the original process. The suspension, the intervention, and the restoration were all alike miraculous in nature. The action of God might thus be compared to one of the great rotary presses used in the production of modern newspapers. Each sentence of the newspaper is fixed in advance and goes over the rollers unaltered if there is no interference, but if the editor decides that a particularly urgent paragraph must go in at the last moment, the rotating machine is stopped, the new paragraph is inserted into the text, and the machine rolls on once more.

This is the version of miracles which was born out of the conflict between religion and the deterministic world view of natural science. But if the universe can no longer be likened to a mechanical printing press, this whole explanation of miracle is irrelevant, and the seeming contradiction between natural causes on the one hand and the will of God on the other is no longer necessary.

Furthermore, facts would seem to suggest that 'the faith which moves mountains' is not limited to specifically 'religious' or 'spiritual' activities. (Indeed, to seek to remove a mountain is not a particularly spiritual activity anyhow.) The contrast often drawn between natural and supernatural events must be abandoned, for everything that happens happens naturally if God is the Creator and Ruler of nature. The 'miracle' of the fakir and the faith healer and the miracles of the Gospel are all natural in that they reveal something of the inner structure of the universe. We need no longer hold miracles and natural causes in antithesis. But I believe we can move beyond this relative distinction in thought only on the assumption of another dimension or a higher unity which holds both the material and the spiritual in one existence.

Certainly the miracle stories of the Gospels do not give the impression that Jesus was a Very Ingenious Person halting the mechanism of a rotary machine in order to effect a change before the process continued. All the miracle stories can be much more acceptably explained by an activity in which will influences material circumstances. In the dramatic climax of the story in Mark 9, when, in their Master's absence, the disciples fail to heal a 'possessed' youth, Jesus returns and expresses His emotion in the strongest terms: 'O faithless generation, how long shall I be with you? how long shall I bear with you? bring him unto me!' This rebuke is not directed to any ignorance of how to manipulate physical things, but to a lack of personal ability to face an enemy which was overcome when once Christ Himself took the field.

There is always something very mysterious about the human, everyday acts of will whereby our minds order our hands to take hold of a pen, to write a sentence on paper, or to strike the keys of a piano. Up to a point we are able to trace the course of the waves propagated in our bodies when the motor nerves are stimulated from the cerebral cortex and a corresponding muscular reaction is evoked, but it is beyond our understanding to say clearly how this wave movement is initiated and what invisible centre of command gives the order which our muscles obey. Yet if as a healthy man I give the order to carry out a particular movement to my hand or foot, it will be obeyed.

A person under hypnosis told that he has been stung by a wasp immediately suffers a swelling on his skin which exactly corresponds to a wasp sting. Blisters can be produced by the same means. This undoubted influence of psychic force may well prove to be an important clue to the understanding of irregular and unorthodox healing which people still call 'miraculous'. There is a growing volume of evidence to suggest that some organic as well as nervous diseases may be induced and healed by psychic means.

In Mark 11[23] Jesus does not say that a particular man can transfer a mountain into the sea by uttering a magic word, but He does say that only if every trace of doubt is banished from a man's mind and heart in respect of a certain event can it happen, and that when such doubt is removed 'miraculous' things can take place within God's purpose. Clearly no one would utter such a ridiculous command as to order a mountain into the sea without entertaining some doubts as to its accomplishment, but the things which *are* within God's purpose depend for their fulfilment upon this 'nothing doubting'.

Is physical health and personal wellbeing within the purpose of

God? Are 'health' and 'salvation' complementary if not synonymous words? The New Testament seems to give a clear answer when we do not look at it through spectacles of which one lens sees 'God's will' and the other 'natural causes'! Consider the following facts:

Jesus affirmed that He had come to do the will of God (Jn 6[38]).

Jesus healed the sick, showing that it is the will of God that people should be well (Lk 9[11]).

Jesus told His disciples to heal the sick (Lk 10[9]).

Jesus said that those who followed Him should do the works that He did and even greater ones, because He was going to the Father and would send the Holy Spirit (Jn 14[12]).

Jesus told us to ask for what we wanted, and that we should receive it (Mk 7[7]).

Jesus told us to pray in faith, believing that God would answer our prayers (Mt 21[22]).

The Old Testament passages which Jesus said He came to fulfil include such physical things as the cure of diseases (Mt 8[17]).

Prayer for the healing of the sick is commended in James 5[16] and the author affirms that believing is a way to becoming well again (James 5[15]).

There would seem to be no evidence in the New Testament that disease is part of God's intention for man. Our illnesses, like our sins, may be held to come from unhealthy conditions in the world around us, our own inner weaknesses, or perhaps most of all from our own wrong attitudes of mind and unhealthy ways of living.

Now behind the work of the medical profession and of our own attitude to sickness and disease, are certain fundamental assumptions without which no one would ever become a doctor or a nurse, or even bother to seek healing for their friends. These assumptions are that disease is evil and should be cured, that health is good and should be fostered, that mental attitudes are most important even in physical disease, that the work of healing is a moral obligation, and that love is a therapeutic agent. Every one of these assumptions is grounded in the theology of the Christian Gospel, and if they now seem to belong to all civilized people, it is largely a gift to man from the Christian Faith.

It may then be affirmed that the words 'health' and 'salvation' should be regarded as complimentary expressions of God's loving will for man, and should continue to characterize the Christian mission and message to the world.

Finally, it may be affirmed that this thesis can be confirmed by experiment when, alone or in fellowship, people follow that way of prayer which is consistent with certain fundamental beliefs.

We do not pray because God needs to be reminded of us or of our symptoms. No prayers we offer can make Him love us more than He does already, and nothing that we can say to Him can deepen His desire that we should have life abundantly. Indeed, long before we begin to pray, God is actively at work in our lives seeking to make them whole. So our prayer should first of all be such an awareness of this fact that we want to thank God for His present goodness and love to us in nature and by grace. This glad awareness of God's healing presence in our lives leads to a deep and genuine penitence when we begin to wish to know the ways in which we have failed to understand His purpose in our lives. If His will is for our health as well as for our holiness, some habit of thought or way of life may well be hindering the inflowing of life abundant. If we ask Him simply and expectantly, I believe that He will show us where we have been in the wrong and where we need His forgiveness.

The second fundamental belief on which prayer for wholeness of life should be based concerns the intimate relationships which exist between body and soul. If the main aim of prayer is reverence for a superior, then to kneel or to prostrate oneself helps to induce the desired attitude of mind and soul. But if our main need is to receive the good gifts God is waiting to give our posture should, be one in which we can relax those muscular tensions which of themselves induce so much dis-ease of stress and strain. As certain diseases and disorders can be cured simply by learning how to relax, so the technique of relaxation is a valuable introduction to this way of prayer. Until we learn it we have no idea of the grim and tense determination with which we frequently attack the life of devotion. We can neither receive nor share the peace of God if we go about life with our jaws set tightly and our muscles so taut that we give ourselves nervous indigestion.

Finally, we must rediscover a way of prayer in which the Holy Spirit can be enabled to invade and inhabit those lower levels of our being which in psychological mythology are called the subconscious and unconscious mind. If all sorts of evil influences can attack our wellbeing at those levels, it is equally possible for God Himself to build us up from the inner man. When a man is in Christ Jesus there is a new creation, and in that new life we learn to breathe in and rest upon these fundamental truths of our Christian faith.

So before you begin to think or say any formal prayers, relax physically. Sit comfortably in your chair with both feet on the ground, your back straight and your eyes closed; or lie quite still on your back. Release all tensions in your muscles—your legs, arms, neck, face and head. Take a few deep breaths to help you be calm and relaxed, and let go all tensions and physical strain. In that spirit of rest turn your mind to God and prayer.

First think of God. Remember He is always where you are and in your heart. 'He is not far from any one of us, for in Him we live and move and have our being.' God is love and light and life, and like the air we breathe is both around us and within. So take one affirmation of the Gospel, such as the text, 'I came that they might have life ... abundantly', and in this mood of relaxed awareness of God's presence repeat it to yourself until it really sinks into your mind and you so truly accept it that you become increasingly assured that God is working out His purpose of fullness of life in you. Such awareness will not necessarily come all at once, and you will need to learn this way of praying until you can pray without ceasing. Those who do so find it abundantly rewarding. A fellow minister wrote the other day: 'I have been reading and thinking and praying along these lines for the last five or six years, and as a result I have found my life completely revolutionized.' Those who follow this way of prayer will be enabled to discover ever-increasing richness in the familiar hymn:

> Praise to the Lord, the Almighty,
>   the King of Creation,
> O my soul praise Him, for He is
>   thy *health and salvation*.

7
The Psychology of Healing
Percy L. Backus

THE PSYCHOLOGY OF HEALING

As THE TITLE suggests, it will be my attempt to present in this chapter the psychological factors that contribute to, or delay, the process of healing, as we understand the facts today. Healing is to be considered in terms of the whole man—spirit, mind, and body. It will be observed that the mind falls midway in this concept of the whole man; and therefore, as the seat, so to speak, of the psychological processes, it will be our study to consider it, not only in relationship to mind processes in themselves, but in the effect of these on both body and spirit. Also, we must study the reverse effects of disorders of the body or the spirit on the mind. It is hoped that by giving consideration to this aspect of healing we may come into a better understanding of our own inner tensions, and have a better appreciation of our relations with others.

The problem of dis-ease presents itself by the introduction of disturbing or harmful forces coming from within and from without. Those that are apparently from within the self are often the result of earlier invasions of some form of environmental stress or disturbance. For example, in early childhood a lack of understanding, a withdrawal of love in situations of pain or distress, a too demanding restraint, ridicule, excessive sympathy—all these can contribute to a wrong conditioning of the child to the problem of pain or frustration. Such disordered functioning of relationships inevitably produces a symptomatology associated with discomfort or pain, which is the normal signal in the mind whereby we become aware of the disorder. Without this warning symptomatology, which may range from discomfort to severe pain, physically, mentally, or in the spirit, we should soon be the victims of severe disease; indeed this protective mechanism often does fail in its beginnings, and so does not operate in time to save us from severe illness. More often by far, the neglect of a warning symptomatology leads to greater distress. If we could only recognize truth more easily and be obedient to its revelation, from how much illness should we be saved! Full health is that state wherein all the functions of body and mind operate in co-ordination with each other up to a satisfactory and sustained level; this gives to the mind a feeling of integrated wholeness and comfort, which in turn, when accompanied with a reasonable sense of relationship to values in the spirit, helps us to live and act at the level of our truer insights.

Let us first consider the needs of the body. Protective care, as we can see when we consider the new-born infant, must come first. Food of the right quantity and nature to supply the needs of our physiological requirements during growth and life comes next. Exercise, to assist in the development of the body and its growth, with the maintenance of its full function throughout life, accompanies these two. As a complement to these, periods of complete rest are essential. In dis-ease, special consideration of all these aspects of the bodily needs is required. This presents the barest outline of the basic needs of the body, the self in a physical sense.

The same brief outline can be applied to the mind—protective care, food, exercise, and rest. In dis-ease, these also require special consideration. But since the mind is, as it were, the initiator and the regulator in such large measure not only of itself, but of the body as well, it is essential to have some understanding of how it develops and functions.

The brain, the seat of control in the mind, is formed embryonically by an infolding of the ectoderm, or outer layer of the embryo, during its first days of existence. Thus the brain and the skin are of the same embryonic origin. No wonder our skin, which is our outer covering to meet the world, is so responsive to the state of our mind in our relationships and reactions.

The pathways in the brain are incomplete at birth, but by six months of age they are sufficiently established for co-ordination of function, that is, for co-ordinated movement to begin to show itself. However, the full development of the brain cells is not reached until about fourteen years of age, when we probably have them all. The development and use of them is a matter of experience and education, which may continue through life, but declines in learning power with advancing years—in some earlier than others. Some areas of the brain have special functions, but others appear to have no localized special expression, so that even when part of the brain becomes damaged, the brain still carries on with apparently little, if any, diminution of ability. If there is temporary loss of function, this appears to be taken over by other parts of the brain. Thus certain diseases of the brain may not show themselves for some time. On the other hand, inherited disease, excessive trauma at birth, illnesses in infancy or childhood, may all so affect the brain as seriously to limit its development and function, both physically and mentally.

A word needs to be added here about inheritance. The genes, or inheritance substance of the reproductive cell, is a part of all that has gone before it; sometimes reinforcing, at other times reducing all the product of change through the union of the two reproductive cells, male and female. They in turn, as the result of the evolution of man, are gradually but surely affected by external, or environmental forces. Sudden or spectacular changes known as mutations do occur.

In the human embryo of today there are visible signs of the bodily structure of our pre-human heritage. It is also true that the oldest part of our brain structure is proved still to be the seat of our primitive physical responses. This part of the brain is also the centre of the automatic control of our bodily organs and blood vessels. The blush response, the effect of fear, and all the physiological reactions thereto, such as the increased heart beat, disturbed digestion, are examples of this.

This part of the brain is also directly connected with the pituitary body, or chief regulator of the special internal glandular system of the body, again reinforcing or diminishing bodily function in many ways.

Other parts of the brain have to do with willed control, but this too may be so disturbed by physical or functional disease as to produce a quite abnormal activity, or on the other hand, to suspend it altogether.

The mind of the infant is essentially self-centred, being possessed by the self's biological needs and comforts. This must be, for its preservation. If development is normal, by about seven years of age the power to appreciate thought begins, and so values emerge in an inner sense, rather than by external pressures. Though values may be described by the child as 'right' and 'wrong', because of concepts given by those who teach the child, these values are simply 'good' and 'bad'. An inner consciousness, capable of analysis on its own merits, has not yet adequately emerged within the mind. Hence, the very great importance during this period of the teaching of values, by precept and example, in the home. The infant, even at his biological stage, responds, as we so well know, to the kind of care he gets in protection and food requirements. Faulty supply may start patterns of response that will still show themselves in adult life. An analysis in the adult responses by the use of phantasy formation may lead directly back to such early experiences of which there is no memory. Being wanted, loved, and properly fed, preferably at the mother's breast, even if the feeding must be artificial, is very different in its effect from being unwanted, unloved, and pushed away into a cot to struggle alone with a bottle of unsuitable food at the wrong temperature. Even the care of the bath and the bowels is important. But above all, the love relationship is the most important.

All this will have a profound effect on the infant's emotional development and response. Thus, the unloved, unwanted infant and child may suffer so much from deprivation that he will react, according to the inherited characteristics of temperament, by abnormal fears and anxiety, or by rebellion and hate. These so-called ambivalent swings of love and hate in early childhood, if not properly understood by the parents, may result in disaster for the child.

The basic patterns of reaction, though modifiable in later life, are essentially laid down during these early years of experience and training, before the individual assessment of values is reached at seven years of age. Thus, the saying 'Bring up a child in the way he should go, and then when he is old he will not depart from it' is fundamentally true. What it is necessary to know is how he should be brought up.

This bringing up is thus a vital thing. Relationships are of the greatest importance. The relationship of the child to parents (especially the mother when the child is young), the relationship of the parents to one another, and the total family relationship of each member to the other, become matters for prominent consideration.

Inherited characteristics may be said to have to do with the temperament; calm or excitable, stolid or sensitive, phlegmatic or easily moved, these things are of importance. Again, we may be described as introverted or extroverted—withdrawn or ready to express ourselves freely, quiet and rather reserved, or the 'life and soul' of the party. Temperament may be considered as a spectrum band, with introversion at one end and extroversions at the other. Fortunate is he who finds himself midway between each extreme; and more fortunate still is he who has had the upbringing that gives him a wide expanse in this spectrum. To be at times quiet, thoughtful, reserved, capable of good appreciation of others and possessing inner control, and to be at other times ready and able to give oneself freely and spontaneously, not always counting the cost, is evidence of a breadth of personality for which to be thankful.

Generally speaking, if emotional conflicts arise, the introverted child becomes anxious and full of fear; he suffers from an Anxiety State. In similar circumstances the extrovert tends to externalize his symptoms and produce a symptomatology to cover up his trouble—he becomes a Hysteric. He who falls midway may show symptoms of anxiety, or hysteria, or both.

The conflict may be dealt with by repression, which is an unconscious mental mechanism, and is held down with much unconscious emotional tension as an Anxiety; or it may escape as a conscious symptom, and free the patient from internal tension. In the former, the patient becomes anxious and tense, with all the symptomatology that goes with a normal fear reaction, and when chronic in form this may produce bodily change of pathological intensity. In the latter, the symptom or symptoms affect the function of the body in varying degrees, and cause loss or exaggeration of function, and may simulate almost any known disease—such as spasm, or paresis of parts of the body, blindness, deafness, inability to use muscles properly, altered functions of organs, sensory disturbances such as loss of sensation, or unusual pains and quite abnormal fears not at all understood by the patient.

The patterns for these reactions are laid down in early childhood and added to by subsequent experiences in life. It is equally true that proper upbringing, with a recognition of these difficulties, may correct such abnormalities and thus save the child from a later neurosis. The timid child may be helped to become brave; the frightened, insecure child may be helped to security. The child of over-indulgence may learn balance in contact with others. The primary remedy lies in stable parents who have found balance in their own lives, together with a good relationship between them in their marriage.

Where difficulties in the home relationship exist, what are the consequences? The ego development of the child, to begin with, depends upon security and care. This is soon dominated by parental and other controls, which, when too demanding and severe, so strengthen the superego, or conscience, that the child becomes the slave of imposed rule or law. This limits, or canalizes the inner development, and leads to a restricted type of individual, full of prejudices and hyper-criticism of the self, with its projection on to others; a slavish submissiveness to others may result, or the opposite in the more aggressive types, leading to intolerance. On the other hand, a too indulgent and over protective attitude leads to self-indulgence, excessive demand, and a failure to accept responsibility for the self as well as in relationship with others. This in turn retards emotional development; and immaturity, with its consequent attitude to disease, remains.

These attitudes, when reinforced by the social attitudes of the parents, whether generous, restricted or anti-social, diminish or aggravate the behaviour of the child, and patterns of behaviour develop accordingly. When school is added to the experience of the child, these attitudes will be further modified by companionship with other children and the leadership given by the teacher.

While this is happening, aggressive drives within the child are developing as part of his biological emergence. If these are suppressed, new conflicts will arise in reaction to them. If they are allowed to develop without some helpful discipline, the child becomes the victim of his own impulses, over which he has no adequate emotional control because of his immaturity. These disciplines, when taken over by the child, contribute to the development of his own conscience (or superego, to use the technical phrase). Failure in this, or a too rigid acceptance, creates conflicts that may emerge in later life as a neurosis when the environmental stresses are too severe. The possessive, or over-strict parent is liable to produce the obsessional child, who will suffer from various phobias, usually related to the early experiences of life.

Physical illness too, in childhood, if not wisely handled, can become a source of future conflict in which the physical is added to the mental in the causation of emotional disease.

Finally, there are the moral issues, based upon spiritual values. If these are totally neglected, then the child tends to develop along biological lines, in which the self is essentially the only object of consideration. Relationships with others are considered only in so far as those relationships may be thought to be of value to the self.

From what has already been said, it is not difficult to see that in any treatment whatever of the adult, these basic factors must be recognized, and understood in their far-reaching consequences. Not to understand here is to attempt to treat the branch symptom and not the root cause of the trouble, thus leaving a hidden, deep-seated source of future difficulty.

What then are the requirements of the physician who seeks to treat such patients?

He needs to have extensive knowledge and understanding of physical illnesses, their causes as well as their effects, or, failing this, he needs to be closely allied in his work with someone who has.

He also needs a full understanding of the psychological principles that are involved in the activity of the mind. He needs to have his own psychological processes fully investigated and understood, so that he has no 'blind spots' in his understanding of himself that may affect the treatment of others.

Finally, he needs to be fully aware of values, and seek to practise them, so that he shall do no harm to the total structure of the patient's personality.

The life instinct, so called, is at the beginning of emotional development. The only other major instinct is the sex instinct, which, though present in early life, makes itself much more actively manifest at puberty, when the emotional state of the individual is still not sufficiently mature to cope satisfactorily with it. We therefore mature biologically before we do so emotionally, and in turn, we mature emotionally before we have taken into our personality an adequate sense of values and a fully developed idealism. This latter may never be complete, and thus complicates the treatment. Sometimes it is not sufficiently complete in the physician himself. The total personality needs to be considered at all times. Values must then be positive, not negative, and need to be great enough to capture the imagination, and thereby win the allegiance of the individual for their own sake. This leads us to a consideration of this transformation.

During mental and emotional growth, the values of the 'rules' and 'laws' in life become evident, and may be accepted. The guidance of the biological urges may be achieved, but unless their inherent moral and spiritual value is fully understood, appreciated, and desired, no real change takes place. The individual is still under the Law. Good and necessary as that may be in many instances and situations, it does not free the patient of his illness. His symptoms may be relieved, but that is not enough.

A totally exaggerated sense of values, quite beyond the attainment of the individual at this time, may be held, and requires to be understood. On the other hand, a toning down of values, such as would make the biological urges of the individual acceptable at levels below the considered moral standard of the patient, can be disastrous. Symptoms may be relieved thereby, but again the patient is not cured. It may take many sessions to draw out of the patient a sufficient understanding of his difficulties and the underlying causes of them.

Until the 'rules' or 'laws of life' become the 'wants' of life, something to be infinitely desired, and the patient has a real desire towards the fulfilment of his values, he will not be fundamentally healed, that is, integrated, whole. Should the values which the patient holds be too low for his needs, he usually becomes aware of this, and seeks to correct it, because right values now become a 'want' and not a 'must'. At heart, the patient wants health, to be whole. He wants life, and indeed, he wants it more abundantly. Until this want is fundamental, healing cannot be complete. The question of Jesus, 'Wouldest thou be made whole?' is basic. If the process of these sessions unfolds an analysis of the patient's illness, and awakens his desire to be whole, there should follow an integration of his self sufficient to enable him to live happily, not only with himself, but also with all others.

In order to help the many who want to be whole, there is a great need for those who are willing to be equipped to share in team work to this end.

The general practitioner, as the family physician, is one of a great company who, in the prevention and treatment of disease, is giving humanity noble service; he is the 'salt of the earth'. He has the opportunity of knowing the whole man in his particular environment, and is therefore the first in the field to help. Unfortunately, too often, lack of adequate time prevents him from serving as he would.

To assist him in his more complex and difficult situations he has the help of a consultant and specialist service, but these can never replace the valuable help he gives. He is bound to be uniquely aware of much of the mental and spiritual need of his patients, and indeed, by example and advice, can give much valuable psychological treatment and sustain a real sense of values.

The consultant physician in psychological medicine may advise, and, like other specialists, may have to treat in his own field, but he too needs to know his whole patient in his total setting, the self and its environment. He thus needs to know the physical facts, or have close co-operation with one who does, though his special field consists of the problems of the mind, which include the emotions.

What has been said about the medical profession, can also be applied to the clergy, of whom so many have felt the call to give time and study to the ministry of healing, many of them in the field of emotional difficulties alone, and some in the realms where ill-health is mental and physical. Into this team must come the clergy, for without their presentation of values and understanding of the way of attainment, there can be no lasting benefit in the treatment. The superego, or conscience, with its strong critical sense, must be related to an idealism and a fulfilment which, I believe, has its source in God Himself. Only so will there be peace within the heart, a forgiving tolerance of others, and a readiness to spend the self in meeting the needs of others; only so will the patient learn to love his neighbour to a point approaching as nearly as possible the love of himself.

There is one other field, that of the psychoses, the troubles which afflict the mentally deranged. The treatment of these is as highly specialized as any specialism; and, though they are usually recognizable, this is the field of work of the highly trained specialist and no other, though ancillary help under his guidance may be of value from us all. In the new Mental Health Act there is provision for such ancillary treatment in other environments than the mental hospital. This, too, will call for much understanding, tolerance, and love.

In close relationship with these illnesses, is that of depression. All such cases must be taken seriously, because, with the treatments now available, and the care of expert hands, casualties become increasingly rare. No form of depression should be left today to recover on its own, even if cyclical in type.

At the heart of all development, and if needed, treatment, lies a loving relationship properly understood and rightly applied. This, with a knowledge of the truth about the patient from childhood, will often succeed in preventing neurosis, and in curing it where it exists. But this needs always to be integrated into a desire for values, a goal seen that is adequate for the person's needs, a love relationship with society as a whole, and above all with the Source of all loving.

The way of development of the whole self, biological, mental, spiritual, must always be our concern. The right understanding and application of values in this development must follow, if the self is to mature to the fullness of its stature, because in the end values are the only things that count, the only things that remain with us as gifts from their true Source, God, who is our Father. To me their greatest revelation comes through a search for a proper understanding of them as revealed in Christ. This objective becomes supreme, because no other equals it. It can become the supreme ego idealism that lifts us through high endeavour to peace and joy, and some measure of our fulfilment of God's purpose for us in a creation of which we are a part.

8
Healing and the Minister
Reginald Brighton

HEALING AND THE MINISTER

INTRODUCTION
THE CHALLENGE TO HEAL

THERE IS A sense in which this whole book deals with the subject of 'Healing and the Minister'. This present essay seeks to deal with the matter of ministerial responsibility, approach and practical out-working in the field of healing. It looks at it from the standpoint of the minister who has probably had little or no guidance on healing in his theological training and finds himself facing the practical issues in his day-to-day work.

For no minister will have gone far in his ministry today before he is confronted with the challenge to heal. It will come to him from several quarters and the conscientious man will not be able to ignore so persistent a question. What he is to think and do will be a living issue with him.

The challenge will come first of all from the New Testament. What is he to make of the healing ministry of Jesus, His commission to heal and the continued healing ministry of the Apostolic Church? Can all this be ignored on theological grounds or set aside on grounds of historical criticism? The conscientious minister knows very well that it cannot and that here lies an issue and a challenge to him and his ministry.

There may be exceptions to this in men who are able to believe that the healing miracles of Jesus were for the purpose of establishing the fact of the deity of Christ to His contemporaries! They may be able to accept that the healing miracles were in the nature of a short-term divine strategy and that the Church would lose in due time its healing ministry.[1] They may be able to accept, too (as I think they logically must), the traditional dichotomy of body and soul, and be content to leave the body to the doctors and rest satisfied with an exclusive claim to the soul.

[1] A view represented by *Some Thoughts on Faith Healing*, edited by Vincent Edmunds, M.D., M.R.C.P., and C. Gordon Scorer, M.B.E., M.A., M.D., F.R.C.S. (Tyndale Press, 1956).

But for most men who have been trained in the more liberal and modern schools, such theology is untenable and the challenge of the New Testament to heal remains a very real issue.

But this challenge does not stand alone. There is the challenge of actual sickness. The minister finds himself confronted by people who are ill and whose illnesses take every conceivable form from emotional maladjustment and moral defeat to the last stages of cancer and other diseases of doom. What is his attitude to be? Just what is he expected to do? Can he make a sharp distinction between the moral and psychological problems which confront him, deal with the former on the basis of his theological knowledge and leave the latter to the psychiatrist? What can he do when he visits the sick? Is it enough just to pray with the sick person? Is there no ministry of healing anywhere along the line?

In this situation there is yet another challenge, that of the healer and the healing sects. What assessment is to be made of men like Harry Edwards in England and Oral Roberts in America? How is the minister to regard the claims of Christian Science and spiritualistic healers? Is he being fair if he regards such ministries as fanatical and unworthy of consideration?

Christian Science and Spiritualism have been fairly dealt with by Dr Leslie Weatherhead[2] and others. Not so much has been written about individual healers, and it is not easy to assess them and their work. What is obvious to the minister is that there is a field of non-physical healing, that it extends beyond the sphere of orthodox medicine, and that religion and religious factors like faith are involved. Where does he come in? Should he expect to be a faith healer? Should he expect to have a healing gift? Do the sects and cults point a way that orthodox Christianity has lost?

The challenge to heal comes to the minister not only from the New Testament, the presence of illness all around him, and the many claims which are made by healers, cults and sects, but from quite a different quarter today. He cannot be blind to the new understanding alike of illness and health which have come through psychology and psychosomatic medicine. The former has revealed the inter-action of mind and body, and the latter has shown the extent to which this is operative in illnesses once thought to be entirely physical in nature and origin. The conclusion to be drawn is that man is far more a unity of physical, mental and spiritual

[2] In addition to the chapter in this present book, see *Psychology, Religion and Healing* (Hodder & Stoughton, 1951).

HEALING AND THE MINISTER 139

functioning than has ever been realized.[3] The implication for the minister is that there can be no consideration of illness or health which does not touch upon religion. Always there are moral and spiritual factors. Whether he likes it or not, the minister is involved. He can sit back and ignore the fact that people with their guilt and consequent unhappiness are going to doctors and psychiatrists. He can ignore the reports that more Protestants find their way there than Roman Catholics,[4] who have their own means of confession and absolution. But there is no doubt about the challenge of the situation. The modern minister faces a situation undreamed-of by his counterpart of two generations or even one generation ago. He is faced with a great question-mark. For this is not only a matter of challenge but of new opportunity and new relevance. The modern minister must make up his mind about his healing ministry.

I

APPROACH AND INTERPRETATION

It might seem that the question would be answered if the minister found himself the possessor of some healing gift. That there are people so endowed, and that the gift is a natural one, is beyond much doubt. It is also in little doubt that a clear distinction must be drawn between the fact of the gift and the explanation of it given by its possessor. There are those who say their gift is the work of spirit guides, others who put it into a Christian context and attribute it to the Holy Spirit, yet others work it out in terms of radiaesthesia or odic force.[5] It would seem that there is a natural gift of a psychic order, varying in degree and in comprehensiveness from person to person, and capable perhaps of development according to the character of the individual. If a minister were so endowed, and dedicated his gift to the service of God and man,

---

[3] It is significant that the most positive aspect of the Church's position in the report of the Archbishop's Commission, *The Church's Ministry of Healing*, is based upon the assumption of the essential unity of man. Note particularly p. 11, para 6; p. 16, para. 16; and pp. 56–7, paras. 121–2.
[4] C. G. Jung, in *Modern Man in Search of a Soul* (Kegan Paul, 1945 edn.), p. 264.
[5] In our own day these attitudes are represented by Mr Harry Edwards, Mrs Elsie Salmon, Dr Michael Ash, and Dr Leslie Weatherhead respectively.

would that meet the situation we have described and fulfil his healing vocation today?

The answer, surely, is that such a gift could be helpful if it were wisely used. But unless the minister's healing task is to be thought of in other and different terms, many would be excluded from it altogether, for only few have any such gift. Whatever the healing mission of the minister, it must be one which is broadly applicable to all and should arise out of his normal ministerial vocation.

This surely is the perspective of the New Testament in general and of St Paul in particular. The primary ministry of the Church was the work of the apostle; the function of special gifts was secondary, and indeed 'gifts of healings' come fifth on St Paul's list (1 Cor 12^8). The big question before us as ministers concerns the nature of our primary, apostolic ministry, and whether it contains a healing ministry apart altogether from the healing gift.

The apostolic function is the mediation of the Gospel. The Gospel is to be found among the primary concepts of the New Testament. In the synoptic Gospels we have the concept of the Kingdom of God, in St Paul's letters the heart of the matter is the life in Christ, and in the fourth Gospel it is life eternal. We have not here three different Gospels but one, not three different offers of God but one, and all indicate life in a new order, or in a new dimension, offered by God, through Christ, to men. Its result is salvation and this is not only a deliverance from the destructive negations of life, but is a positive wholeness or integration.

What does this mean in terms of health and healing? We must ask this question, not against the background of the ancient dichotomy of body and soul, but in the light of our modern understanding of man as a unity—an organism of inter-acting functioning, physical, mental and spiritual. If man in his essential being, in his relationship with God, is changed, and if in that dimension of his life there is a new alignment and a new unity, this must have a profound effect upon mind and body.

The writer was present at a conference of ministers and doctors when a well-known surgeon said to the ministers present: 'If you men only do your job you are the greatest factor in preventive medicine there is in the world!'[6] I interpreted him as meaning that if we really restored men to God through the preaching and ministry of the Christian Gospel, we should be going a long way

---

[6] I quote from memory. The speaker was Mr Arthur Hill.

towards solving the human problems of guilt and fear, and should be creating a new wholeness in the human personality.

The important thing is that there is a ministry of healing, a ministry which is quite incalculable, in the essential ministry of the Christian Church. It is to be seen not only in the way of preventive medicine, as bringing men into a condition of being in which illness is less likely, but also in the way of bringing to illness new factors of healing. It can help the patient to the right attitude to his illness. It can surround him, and those who are medically responsible for him, with the influence and power of that 'other dimension' with which the Gospel is concerned. It can render positive any situation of illness, which would otherwise be quite negative and destructive in its outcome. Just as death itself is transformed in the setting of the Gospel, so also is illness, even when the outcome is not the restoration of physical health. The essential ministry of the Christian Church enhances the possibility of physical health and healing because its concern is with the total health and healing of the human being.

For this reason the minister pursues his ministry of healing when he seeks to make the Church the Church. This is never an easy task because the Church finds it extremely easy to become a '*this*-dimensional' organization, as Dr Paul Tillich has put it, 'horizontal' instead of 'vertical'.[7] But there is no question that the minister participates in his true healing ministry when he seeks to make his local Church, through ministry of Word and Sacrament, through creation of units of fellowship and prayer, and through his personal pastoral ministry, a therapeutic community. And here, in the view of the writer, lies the answer to much of the Church's supposed irrelevance today, as well as to the question of the nature of the minister's essential healing vocation.

2

PRACTICAL OUTWORKINGS

THE minister's main task is to make the Church the Church through the ministry of Word and Sacraments, through creating units of fellowship and prayer, and through his personal pastoral ministry. It is in the last that his more specialized and personal healing ministry takes its shape, though it can never be considered

[7] Article in the *Saturday Evening Post* (June 1958).

by itself; it is always part of the much larger whole. The manner and extent to which people will come to him personally will be determined by the character of his entire ministry. If his Church is on a rising tide of spiritual life, there will be an increasing number who will look to him for spiritual direction. The better known he is in the community generally, the more people will come to him with their personal problems. The character of the local Church will determine much in respect of his personal ministry.

But so also will the personal, pastoral ministry have a definite bearing on the local Church. It is with the pattern of this ministry that we are primarily concerned. Here is the minister's personal and individual sphere of healing. It divides itself into three parts—
(*a*) Spiritual direction.
(*b*) Visitation of the sick.
(*c*) Dealing with personal problems.
Obviously each of these has a bearing on the others, but they have to be separated if they are to be seen and understood, and different factors are involved in each.

(*a*) *Spiritual Direction*

In the Catholic tradition a distinction is made between auricular confession and spiritual direction. In our Protestant ministry we have no such distinction for we have no 'confessional'. This situation is deplored by an increasing number of Protestants as the value of confession from the standpoint of therapy becomes realized.[8] None the less there are those who make their way to the minister with their spiritual desires and difficulties. This is particularly true when a Church is a living organism of spiritual life. The minister then participates in healing in its most traditional religious form—'the cure of souls'.

It is true that the word 'cure' means strictly 'care', but none the less, as John T. McNeill points out in his *History of the Cure of Souls*, the concept of healing is traditionally present in the use of this time-honoured phrase. Particularly, too, in the light of what we have said about man as a unity, the minister in guiding people in their spiritual desires and difficulties is participating in a very real healing ministry.

[8] Dr George MacLeod in *The Coracle* (March 1959), article on 'Confession and Absolution'.

Those who come to the minister for spiritual guidance can be placed in, broadly, three categories—
(1) Those who have a sense of sin and burden of guilt.
(2) Those who have a more vague and diffuse desire to become Christians.
(3) Those who encounter difficulties in a more mature spiritual life.

Obviously the help that the minister gives must be determined by the nature of the situation and we shall therefore consider each category separately.

(1) *The sense of sin and burden of guilt*

The end in view is clear. It is to bring a seeker to an experience of forgiveness and commitment to Christ. The steps to be taken are reasonably clear and the first is confession. This cannot be done effectively unless there is a relationship of confidence between minister and seeker, and as this depends so much on the minister himself, this matter will be dealt with later in the essay.

The more confession is in the nature of a catharsis the better. It is good that the whole of the story, which may involve a good deal of the seeker's life history, should come out. It must be remembered that this is not taking place within the authoritarian pattern of a Catholic confessional, but in the more friendly, man-to-man relationship which characterizes a Protestant community. The attitude of the minister should always be friendly, understanding and non-judgemental.

Those who have found themselves participating in this kind of ministry will know full well that it is costly—not only for the seeker, but for the minister. It is essentially a relationship of sin-bearing, for the minister shares the humiliation and the pain as the seeker unburdens himself.

None the less, the minister must maintain a certain attitude of detachment. He must not be overwhelmed by what he hears or by the emotional reactions of the person he is helping. Unless he can secure this degree of detachment, he will not keep, as he should, a clear-sighted guidance of the situation.

For vigilance is called for. At this stage the objective is to draw from the seeker a complete confession, added to which there must be a fair assessment of the whole situation. It is here that some psychological knowledge is valuable to the minister. There are mental mechanisms which can be in evidence in the minister's study as well as in the psychiatrist's consulting room. The minister needs to know something of rationalization, displacement and projection, or something less than the real truth will find its way into the confessional situation.

It cannot, I think, be over-emphasized that a confession needs to be full. If it is not, the subsequent healing will not be complete. It needs also to be fairly assessed; if it is not, unreality can militate against future healing. For example, it is possible for the seeker to have a feeling of guilt which is out of all proportion to his wrongdoing. The minister must help the seeker to get fairly adjusted. He must dispel what may be the result of an over-sensitive conscience.

When confession is complete and the material talked about as much as (and not more than) is necessary, the minister's next step is to preach the Gospel to his audience of one. He presents the Cross as God's act in Christ for sinners. Possibly he may share something of his own experience of forgiveness. At all events he makes as clear as he can the source and reality of the forgiveness of God.

It is not, however, sufficient for him simply to show forgiveness objectively. He must go on to mediate forgiveness. The point must be reached at which he can say with meaning and relevance—'Do you accept the forgiveness of all your sins?' This may be done after prayer together. In the experience of the writer, if the previous work has been well done, and if the seeker is a normal person, the response will be 'Yes'. The minister is then in a position to pronounce absolution, and can say, 'In the name of Jesus Christ your sins are forgiven'.

Spiritual direction must, however, continue. The next step is commitment. Christ is not only Saviour; He is Lord. He not only forgives; He guides. He continues to be Saviour, Lord and Guide in relationship. Soon, therefore, the seeker must be asked: 'Do you give yourself back to Him who not only gave Himself for you, but who gives Himself to you?' Again, if the previous work has been well done, the answer will be 'Yes'.

A number of practical considerations must follow. It is necessary to discuss the seeker's life situation in the immediate future—his work, his leisure, and his home. His relationship with the Church must also be talked about, such matters as, for example, Church-membership, Christian service, and—most important—his prayer life.

Needless to say, spiritual direction such as outlined here may take anything from one to four interviews, though it is highly desirable that a person under conviction and after confession should find his peace as soon as possible. And although it is better if an interview does not take longer than one hour, there are situations in which this is quite impossible.

(2) *Diffuse religious desire and aspiration*
Without going too deeply into the question of psychological types and their relation to spiritual experience, there is no doubt that the broad distinction holds between the 'crisis' and 'non-crisis' person.[9] It is essential to distinguish between them in the work of spiritual direction. The 'crisis' person will come to an acute sense of sin, and the method of direction we have already outlined will be right for him; but the 'non-crisis' person will never know any such sharp experience of conviction, and a different approach is necessary. For him the religious situation is far more diffuse. He will probably never know the sudden joy of forgiveness, assurance, and release which the other knows. None the less, he has his hunger and thirst for God, his desire to live a better life, and he will find his way to the minister for help.

Our aim in this situation is to help the inquirer to a growing sense of God and commitment to Him. He must be shown that there are certain 'means of grace' within the Church that are particularly helpful to him, and that in addition, his spiritual growth and inner life depend upon his personal prayer life. Direction therefore should follow three main lines: encouragement to become part of a fellowship unit, instruction in the meaning of Holy Communion, and counsel about the way of personal prayer.

Isolation in the spiritual life must be guarded against. The general life of the Church is the corrective of this, but the particular safeguard is the fellowship group, especially in a living and growing Church. Here the inquirer will take his place, learn to make his contribution in the cut and thrust of discussion, and also learn from others who are in the seeking-finding situation.

The writer was brought-up in a sacramental tradition which was 'memorialist' in its interpretation of Holy Communion. This means of grace was never particularly meaningful or vital to him. It was a looking-back to a great event, indeed the great saving

---

[9] Reference to this is made in *Psychology and Pastoral Practice*, by W. L. Northridge (Epworth Press, 1939), pp. 121-3.

event of the Cross. But it was a looking-back rather than a present realization of the presence of the living Christ. Then came the reading of Dr J. Ernest Rattenbury's *The Eucharistic Hymns of Charles Wesley*, and the understanding of a much fuller meaning of Holy Communion. The bread and wine were the signs not only of Christ's sacrifice but of His presence, and they were the means whereby He was conveyed to the believing heart.

It has seemed to me that instruction which brings out this real value of Holy Communion is of first importance to all seeking Christians, but particularly to the type of which we are now thinking. We speak of him sometimes as the 'quiet, meditative type', and for him the Holy Communion can become the mainstay of the spiritual life.

It is thought by some that teaching about prayer is the essence of spiritual direction, and its value can never be over-estimated. The crux of the whole matter is maturity in prayer, as in every part of life. Fixation in prayer at the level of the child is depicted for ever in William Law's Mundanus, who was grown up in most other things (especially in business method), but still said the prayers he learned from his mother. Helping people to grow-up in their prayer life is the substance of spiritual direction in this matter.

The first stepping-stone is teaching in meditation. It is necessary to help the inquirer to find the right basic book—Bible, hymn-book, devotional manual, ancient or modern. Perhaps only by trial and error will he find the right one. But the main thing is that he shall learn to pick-out the salient verse, phrase or word, and wrest the meaning for himself and apply it to himself. He should be encouraged, too, to realize that he *can do* this, and that such attention is possible for him.

This will lead to direction on the whole problem of distraction—the arch-enemy alike of meditation and all forms of real prayer, and the rock on which are sunk so many voyagers to the land of prayer. It is important that the inquirer should understand that the distraction problem is normal. He should not think he is different from everyone else because he finds attention so difficult; he should realize it is everyman's battle. But he should be given assurance that he can win through, if not to perfection, at least to satisfactory meditation, in the early stages by analysing the content of the distractions, and in the later ones (as *The Cloud of Unknowing* says) by looking over their shoulder.

Instruction in meditation is, however, only a first step in helping an inquirer towards maturity in prayer. He must be shown that prayer begins and ends with God. It is, by the grace of God, self-offering to God, and its end is the uniting of man with God. Meditation, therefore, should lead on from the realizing of truths about God, His goodness, His way of salvation through Christ and other matters pertaining to the Christian Life, to God Himself. The point should be reached at which one is quiet before Him and is lovingly attentive to Him. Some instruction should be given on these higher levels of prayer, variously called 'affective prayer', 'the prayer of quiet' and 'contemplative prayer'. Unless these are understood by the minister, mature and fulfilled prayer is not understood. This means in practice that people cease to pray because they do not realize what a mighty thing prayer is. In fact it is only growing and maturing prayer which is continuing prayer.[10]

From the standpoint of this essay there is even further importance in the true maturing of prayer and its outreach to its true end—the uniting of man with God. That is the relation of this kind of prayer to healing. Much has been made of the 'unity' of man. Here is the place of the *de facto* uniting of man with the Ground of his being. Here is the bringing together of the spirit of man with the Spirit of God—that basic unity which must affect both mind and body. Even more, the masters of prayer tell us that such prayer—contemplative prayer—is far more effective, not only for oneself but also for others, than prayer at the lower levels. The prayer of love directed to God alone, with no words spoken except such single syllable words as 'God', 'Christ', 'Love', flung out in love and longing for Him, can accomplish more than all our petitions and intercessions.[11] Direction, therefore, of the inquirer into the mature sacramental and prayer life of the Christian Church is a normal and effective part of the minister's work in healing.

---

[10] Books which are particularly helpful in this aspect of prayer are *How to Pray*, by Jean-Nicholas Grou (James Clarke), *Elements of the Spiritual Life* (Part IV), by F. P. Harton (S.P.C.K.), and *The Art of Mental Prayer*, by Bede Frost (S.P.C.K.).

[11] This is the standpoint, particularly, of *The Cloud of Unknowing* (Ch. 3): 'This is the work of the soul that most pleaseth God. All saints and angels have joy of this work and hasten them to help it with all their might. All fiends be mad when thou dost thus, and try for to defeat it all they can. All men living on earth be wonderfully helped by this work, thou knowest not how.'

(3) *Difficulties in the spiritual life*

Amongst evangelicals, post-conversion difficulties are not infrequent, especially where there has been a strong emotional content. Repeatedly the minister hears from his inquirers—'I used to feel... now I don't.' Feeling and emotion cannot be eliminated from the religious scene any more than from life itself, but the path of religious experience is from feeling to faith, and to help people in this is the minister's constant task.

To deal with this situation he must understand the many-sided problem of dryness, a condition which afflicts all types of religious people, not only those who are strongly emotional. Dr Herbert Gray in his excellent little book *About People*[12] lists the following eight possible causes—

    (i) Physical unfitness
   (ii) Emotional shock
  (iii) The rhythmic ebb and flow of life
  (iv) Failure to grow-up out of an adolescent religion
   (v) Trying to sustain a wrong religious (denominational) pattern
  (vi) Middle-age doldrums
 (vii) Laziness in religious discipline
(viii) Failure to find adequate Christian service

It is the conviction of Dr Gray, however, that the main cause of dryness is to be found in none of these. It is to be found in plain 'sin'. He says that 'in some respect they are not being quite honest with themselves or with God, and are retaining in their lives some element which they cannot ask God to bless'.[13] This, I imagine, will be a situation understood by all ministers. It will call for a tender and sympathetic handling, and yet at the same time an honest one. So much depends on the individual inquirer. In any event the important thing is to enable him to find his own truth, and guide him through this to the place of forgiveness and restoration.

There is, however, another aspect of this matter with which the minister needs to be familiar, and that is the 'Dark Night of the Soul'. This is a spiritual condition which belongs to Catholic mysticism rather than Evangelical experience. But as in Protestant and Evangelical Churches we have the 'non-crisis' as well as the

[12] S.C.M. (1934).
[13] Op. cit. p. 72.

'crisis' type, so also we have the 'mystical' as well as the 'evangelical', and it is necessary to be able to understand what may be happening in the spiritual life of such a person.

Broadly, the experience of the Dark Night is that which may follow spiritual illumination (the mystical equivalent of evangelical conversion) for the purpose of further purification of the inner-life. Its end is to wean man from dependence on feelings and make it utterly dependent on a sightless, feelingless faith. Man must love God, and Him alone, and for His own sake, and for nothing else under the sun. The process involves an utter stripping, a detachment from all things including the joy and light of illumination. This may well plunge one into darkness, dryness, or what John Wesley called 'the wilderness state', and it must be understood that for *some* this is an essential phase of the spiritual life. It is the contention of Dr H. A. Hodges that John Wesley would have been a wiser man and a better spiritual director had he understood this.[14] Maybe the same must be said of his followers. In any event it would seem to be logical that God cannot really depend upon us unless we *are* prepared to trust Him without benefit of feelings, and that to this end we must go through the darkness. One thing is certain, the minister as director should understand this condition or he may well be guilty of grave misdirection.[15]

But the possibility of misdirection can come from quite another quarter. It is probable that the minister will meet amongst his inquirers those whose mental condition is neither straightforward nor normal. He will be confronted with the mentally ill, people whose anxiety, fear and depression have to be understood in terms of neurosis or psychosis. Ordinary spiritual direction will not meet their case, they require the help of the psychotherapist or psychiatrist. The minister must be able to distinguish this kind of situation when he meets it, and be willing to hand-on his inquirer to someone else. How is he to do this? Only by being acquainted with depth psychology and having a knowledge of psychological medicine.

Of the dangers of psychology to ministers there have been warnings without end over the past quarter of a century. But if the psyche (soul or mind) is not the province of the minister, what is?

---

[14] See *The Way of Integration*, by H. A. Hodges (Spiritual Healing Booklets, No. 3, Epworth Press), p. 36.
[15] Ibid. p. 38.

Surely he should know as much as possible of what scientific investigations can tell him of the functioning of this aspect of human personality? It is his responsibility to be well-read in this subject. How otherwise can he know with what he is dealing? How otherwise can he know when to send an inquirer to a doctor or psychiatrist?

(b) *Visitation of the Sick*

We are not considering this matter from the standpoint of the hospital chaplain, whose ministry is to a wide and varied constituency of people, for whom the problem of initial contact is prominent. Our concern is the work of the local minister who tends his own people in their own homes as well as in various hospitals. For him the contact is, generally speaking, already made, and his ministry is that of meeting the crisis of illness with people he already knows against the background of an already accepted Christianity.

Visitation of the sick is not in the nature of a social call, even though some kinds of pastoral visits may on occasion amount to little else. Here is a situation in which the minister is not only acting in an individual and personal capacity, but as a representative of Christ and the Church. He is taking the resources of the Church to those who are ill, and it is his function to convey those resources, as far as may be possible, to meet their needs.

In this ministry there are no rules. It cannot be laid down what one is to say or do, whether one should always pray with the patient, how long one should stay and so on—the questions often asked by beginners. Each individual patient is different and each set of circumstances is different. What matters is the attitude and aptitude of the minister. In this connection the Americans use the word 'empathy'. By it we are to understand a combination of sympathy, compassion, and rapport. This is essential, but in so far as it covers only the nature of the minister's relationship to the patient, it does not convey the total requirement of the situation. The minister's own spiritual life and relationship with God is the matter of primary importance. There must be sensitivity both to God and man. The minister is the mediator.

It is in this way that the minister is able to convey to the patient those resources and attitudes which he needs either for the restoration of health or to meet the crisis of dying. After all, if the 'other dimensional' forces of the Gospel are real, whose purpose is it to bring them to bear upon the human situation of sickness and death if it is not the minister's? Given this understanding then, he can make his positive and creative contribution in two ways.

(1) He can help the patient to have a right attitude to his illness. There are factors which can seriously retard a person's recovery of health. Some of them come within the province of the psychiatrist but others are within the sphere of the minister. There are matters which are relatively superficial, such as the confident acceptance of a doctor or nurse or hospital, and here quite often the minister can give reassurance. But there are deeper matters—problems of guilt, personal relationships, moral and spiritual slackness and failure.

It is important to keep in mind the end in view, no matter what the problem. This is to bring the patient to an attitude of trust and relaxation. Best of all is to bring him to a condition of repose in Christ. Spiritual direction therefore may be called for, but care should be taken not to over-tax a patient by encouraging a cathartic experience which would be too much for him. Generally speaking suggestion, reassurance and prayer are the means of the most good. Especially is this true of the prayer which brings the realization of Christ's presence and of the quiet which is ours in Him.

(2) The minister can help the patient in the face of death. In this respect the minister has not been helped by the medical attitude which has prevailed during recent years. This has been one of shielding the patient from the thought of death and of encouraging hope even when the end was known to be near. In this situation it has been difficult for the minister to help the patient to face reality. However, there are signs of a change in medical attitude in these days.

Even so, it is possible to prepare the patient for any eventuality without of necessity using the word 'death'. We have noted already that it is our main purpose to bring about an attitude of repose, trust, and tranquillity. This is not done by making promises of recovery and health. Nor is it done by suggesting that faith in Christ will ensure recovery. It is done by helping the patient to put all things in Christ's hands and to trust Him.

The important though paradoxical thing about this Christ-centred attitude of mind and heart is not only that it raises to a maximum the chances and conditions of healing, but also that, if 'the point of no return' has been reached, it makes possible what old-fashioned Methodists used to call 'dying well'. The fact is that whether for life or death it is repose in Christ that matters. It transforms both life and death, sickness and dying. To mediate this is the privilege of the minister.

There is a final factor in the minister's work for the sick which must be mentioned. It has already been emphasized that his work is conditioned by his local Church and that he stands as its representative in relation to the patient. This situation can be appreciated more definitely when the minister has a prayer-fellowship as a centre from which he can operate. Its advantages from the standpoint of an effective pastoral ministry are obvious, but they should be noted.

(1) Names and circumstances of sick and troubled people can be brought to the group for intercession on their behalf. Generally speaking, those whose names are so introduced should be consulted.

(2) The minister will go out into his pastoral work with the spiritual backing and support of (at least) that group.

(3) The pastoral ministry is then being effectively shared by minister and laity.

I have tried to indicate that what we normally call 'the visitation of the sick' is very much more than a friendly call and a prayer by the bedside. It is a positive, 'other dimensional' ministry and could be called (given a right understanding of Christian dying) a ministry of healing in all circumstances.

Certainly there are times when this is not obvious, especially in extreme cases of mental illness and in situations where pain seems to obliterate everything. Co-operation between us and the patient is then at an end. But our ministry is not then at an end. As Christ does for us what we cannot do for ourselves, so we in those circumstances do for the patient what he cannot do for himself. He cannot pray, so we must. The role of the 'suffering servant' is always present in the pastoral ministry, and in no part of it more than in situations of extreme illness.

(c) Dealing with Personal Problems

Whether the minister likes it or not, people will come to him with their personal problems. The extent of their coming will be determined by a number of factors, not least of which is the approachability of the minister himself. Not only that, but there will also be occasions when he must take the initiative. Someone's problem may 'stick out a mile' and the obvious thing is for the minister to suggest that they might have a talk together.

In this field there are three main questions—

(1) Does the minister need psychology?
(2) How can he equip himself?
(3) Is there an interviewing technique?

(1) *Does the minister need psychology?*

When we speak of psychology in this context we mean modern or depth psychology—the accrued results of the work of the three great pioneers, Freud, Adler and Jung. The question can be put in another way—can the minister afford to disregard everything that the scientific investigation of mental and emotional life has revealed over the last half century? And it can be put in yet another way—can he really understand any human problem, whether of sex, fear, inferiority, guilt, scrupulosity, conflict, depression or obsession (to mention only some that he may meet) without taking into account the factor of the 'unconscious'?

The obvious answer is that he can have but the most superficial understanding of human nature and behaviour if the findings of psychology are ignored. What is more, he may become in his dealings with people what some ministers, unfortunately, are— moralistic, authoritarian, dogmatic, and judgemental. For he will not understand human motives, the deep underlying causes of most of the things men do or fail to do.

Let us be more specific. How can the minister understand the all too frequent problem of inferiority without some knowledge of Adler's work? How can he really come to grips with the problems of sex if he discountenances altogether the work of Freud? How can he see what has happened to the over-conscientious and over-scrupulous without some understanding either of Freud's 'superego' or Jung's 'persona' or Adler's 'over-compensation'? Not that he needs to explain such problems to those who have them in the terms of modern psychology, but he does need to understand them himself. Otherwise he will not be able to appreciate what has been happening, and instead of sending some harassed man to a doctor (if he cannot help him himself), will join the chorus of the 'common-sense' people and tell him 'to pull himself together'.

Psychology, then, is necessary to the minister to enable him to understand human nature. It is this which leads Guntrip in his *Psychology for Ministers and Social Workers* to say: 'Psychology is not the concern or monopoly of any one profession. It is the indispensably necessary equipment of all who have to deal with people and their needs and troubles.'[16]

But psychology is necessary to the minister for his personal understanding rather than as a therapeutic technique. The minister is not a psychotherapist. It is not for him to give prolonged analytical treatment to people who suffer with neuroses at great depth in their character pattern. These he should be able to recognize, and should hand on, like those who show symptoms of psychosis, to trained psychotherapists or psychiatrists.

(2) *How can the minister equip himself?*

Preparation is all-important in psychological understanding and for the work of dealing with people. The first essential is for him to understand himself. Mere intellectual knowledge in psychology is as hopeless in dealing with personal problems as mere intellectual knowledge in theology is for the work of spiritual direction. One of the chief values of reading psychology is that the insights so gained may be self-applied. This is all the more important because generally speaking ministers are unable to have the benefit of a 'training-analysis' and the help in self-understanding that this might give. This entire situation reveals the sad fact that ministers have not so far been trained for personal work—neither for spiritual direction nor for sick-visitation nor for dealing with personal problems. Men who are doing this work have had to train themselves. The day will come when this is seen to be a scandal and men will be trained at least as thoroughly for the pastoral as for the preaching office. In the meantime ministers must help themselves, and one of the most valuable means is the application to oneself of the insights given in reading psychology.

Some are afraid of this. Can it not be very overwhelming and lead to morbid introspection and a deal of moral and spiritual bewilderment? The danger must be admitted. But danger can no more be eliminated in adventure which is inward than in that which is outward. Living and growing religion as distinct from rigid morality is dangerous anyway. The vital factor in this situation is Christ Himself. If He is present, whatever psychological

[16] Independent Press (1953 edn.), p. 23.

HEALING AND THE MINISTER 155

insight or honest introspection may reveal, He is always the divine integrating centre. We have always been taught that He is able to deal with sin. In the growing awareness of psychological insights this Gospel is realistically and personally applied. As the minister knows himself and the Christ within, so he is basically equipped to help others through the complexities of their personal problems.

(3) *Is there an interviewing technique?*

We must consider the all-important practical matter of interviewing people. Is there a technique which the minister needs to learn? In the first place a distinction must be drawn between spiritual direction and helping people with their personal problems. The essential difference is in the goal. In spiritual direction the goal has already been consciously chosen or it is already emerging in a person's life pattern; he is already a seeker with a religious end in view. This does not of necessity obtain in the problem situation. A person is problem-conscious rather than goal-conscious, and a different type of approach is called for; indeed the whole matter of counselling technique is raised.

In this field a great deal of work has been done in recent years, particularly in America. Old-established methods have been discarded. This is particularly true of those which could be labelled 'judgemental', and in which it was assumed that the counsellor supplied the answers. They have been replaced by methods which are non-judgemental, non-authoritarian, and non-directive. The best work on the whole subject is Carl R. Rogers's *Counseling and Psychotherapy*, and to this book the writer acknowledges his indebtedness.[17]

Dr Rogers states the nature and aims of counselling as follows: 'Effective counseling consists of a definitely structured, permissive relationship which allows the client to gain an understanding of himself to a degree which enables him to take positive steps in the light of his new orientation.'[18] He gives an account of the relationship and the therapeutic process which takes place in it, which I now give in outline.[19] There are twelve stages—

(1) The individual comes for help. Rightly recognized, this is one

---

[17] Carl R. Rogers, Ph.D., is Professor of Psychology and Psychiatry at the University of Wisconsin, and was formerly Director of the Rochester Guidance Centre. *Counseling and Psychotherapy* was published in 1942 by Houghton Mifflin Company.
[18] Ibid. p. 18.
[19] Ibid. pp. 31ff.

of the most significant steps in therapy. The individual has taken himself in hand, and taken responsible action of the first importance.

(2) The helping situation is usually defined. From the first the client is made aware of the fact that the counselor does not have the answers, but that the counseling situation does provide a place where the client can, with assistance, work out his own solutions to his problems.

(3) The counselor encourages free expression of feelings in regard to the problem. He must permit the flow of hostility and anxiety, the feelings of concern and the feelings of guilt, the ambivalences and the indecisions. . . .

(4) The counselor accepts, recognizes and clarifies these negative feelings. He endeavors by what he says and does to create an atmosphere in which the client can come to recognize that he has these negative feelings and can accept them as a part of himself.

(5) When the individual's negative feelings have been quite fully expressed, they are followed by the faint and tentative expressions of the positive impulses which make for growth.

(6) The counselor accepts and recognizes the positive feelings which are expressed, in the same manner in which he has accepted and recognized the negative feelings. These positive feelings are not accepted with approbation or praise. The positive feelings are accepted as no more and no less a part of the personality than the negative feelings.

(7) This insight, this understanding of the self and acceptance of the self, is the next important aspect of the whole process. It provides the basis on which the individual can go ahead to new levels of integration.

(8) Intermingled with this process of insight is a process of clarification of possible decisions, possible courses of action. The counselor's function here is to help clarify the different choices which might be made.

(9) The initiation of minute, but highly significant, positive actions.

(10) The development of further insight—more complete and accurate self-understanding as the individual gains courage to see more deeply into his own actions.

(11) There is increasingly integrated positive action on the part of the client. There is less fear about making choices, and more confidence in self-directed action. The counselor and client

are now working together in a new sense. The personal relationship between them is at its strongest.
(12) There is a feeling of decreasing need for help and a recognition on the part of the client that the relationship must end.

One final word on problems. Not everyone can be helped by the minister. There are some who will need far more than counselling. This should be detected in the early stages of interviewing, and indeed the minister should never hesitate to pass on to the doctor, psychotherapist, or psychiatrist, people whose needs are beyond his province.

CONCLUSION—THE MINISTER HIMSELF

IT may well be asked about personal work of all types—'Who is sufficient for these things?' Whether we think of spiritual direction, visitation of the sick, or help given to people with personal problems, the same great question mark confronts us. In every case the minister is called to be 'other dimensional'. For the greatest prerequisite of all is a sensitivity to people which depends upon a sensitivity to God.

It may be said that this should naturally arise out of a minister's vocation. Unfortunately, however, he cannot always take himself for granted, and the price of the therapeutic pastoral ministry is constant vigilance in his own spiritual life.

What Catholics have to say to their priests in manuals for directors of souls can be applied to ministers in every aspect of the pastoral ministry. F. P. Harton in his *The Elements of the Spiritual Life* says: 'The priest's whole ability to guide souls depends on his being a man of God. Spiritual guidance can only be undertaken by one who is himself humbly seeking to live with and for God. The direction of souls is the work of the Holy Spirit and the priest is simply the human medium through whom the Spirit works.'[20] Similarly, Bede Frost in *The Art of Mental Prayer* says: 'The office of a director is a subordinate, dependent one; he is no more than an instrument of the One Director, Jesus Christ. His sole work is to wait upon God, to seek to discern the divine will for each soul. Direction is not our own work upon which we invoke the help of God; it is His work which He calls us to aid Him in accomplishing.'[21]

[20] S.P.C.K. (1932), p. 336.
[21] S.P.C.K. (1954), p. 212.

Richard Baxter in *The Reformed Pastor* makes the same kind of emphasis, though from a different point of view. He says: 'See that the work of saving grace be thoroughly wrought in your own souls.' The point is that we cannot guide where we have not been. The director (and the pastoral counsellor) is not a finger-post but a fellow-traveller. Out of his own experiences along the way he is best qualified to help other people.

Christianity is essentially a religion of relationship. The same truth is stated in Buber's frequently quoted phrase: 'All real life is meeting.' This 'meeting' takes place in no human situation more than in the pastoral ministry of the Church. Here, understanding, love and caring are brought to bear on human needs through personal relationships. This is the continuation of the ministry of 'the Suffering Servant', and it constitutes a healing ministry which is indispensable to the life of the world.

9
The Doctor and Healing
Denis V. Martin

THE DOCTOR AND HEALING

THE POST-WAR years have witnessed a rapid and increasing interest in the possibilities of spiritual healing, and the Christian Church in all her denominations is once again seeking to learn the true nature of the healing ministry which was part of the commission of our Lord to His disciples. One of the most encouraging signs of this renewed interest is the increasing extent to which doctors and ministers of religion are meeting one another to discuss ways and means of co-operating in their common task of ministering to the sick, and one of the most important problems that has emerged from these discussions is the urgent need for a clearer understanding of roles and attitudes on both sides. The doctor is often suspicious of any spiritual approach to healing, because of the many uncritical, sentimental and even magical notions that abound today. On the other hand the minister of religion often feels with considerable justification that the scientific training of the doctor has robbed him of any real appreciation of the power of the gospel for healing. This mutual suspicion and distrust is one of the important impediments to progress in a total approach to the sick person today.

A clearer understanding of the doctor's difficulties in accepting a spiritual approach to healing requires, first, a consideration of his training and the effect that this has upon his attitude to disease. Until recent years the approach to the understanding and treatment of disease in our medical schools was given an almost exclusively physical orientation, and today the student still spends the greater part of his time learning about the functioning of the normal body, the pathology of physical disease processes, the techniques of diagnosis, and the many physical remedies that can be applied. Standards are high, the training is long and arduous; but it can be said with considerable confidence that the majority of doctors who qualify in this country are thoroughly competent in their knowledge and application of the physical approach to disease. This heavy weighting of training on the physical side would seem to have been unavoidable because of the rapid increase in the last fifty years of the facts to be learned, and of the materialistic optimism encouraged by the many wonderful discoveries that have been made in the physical sphere. However, such a one-sided approach to the problem has undoubtedly tended to encourage doctors to see and treat disease rather than people, and to discredit instinctively any non-material approach to healing. Lip service has always been paid to the problem of the whole man, but in practice the body has assumed paramount importance.

Nevertheless, in more recent years physiological and psychiatric research have increasingly turned their attention to the effect of the emotional life upon the body. It has been demonstrated that emotions such as fear and rage have a profound effect upon the proper functioning of the physical organs. The development of dynamic psychology has thrown much light upon the nature of unconscious conflict within the mind and its effect upon the body. Our whole understanding of the nature of the functional nervous disorders, or neuroses, has been revolutionized by the research work of the psychoanalysts. Increasingly this new knowledge has been applied to diseases hitherto considered purely 'organic' or 'physical'. There is now generally accepted evidence that emotional conflict plays a part, and sometimes a crucial part, in the causation of much organic disease as well as in the neuroses. These findings have done much to bring general medicine and psychiatry closer together, with the result that the medical student of today has his attention called early to the effect of the mind upon the body, and psychiatry plays a much larger part in his training. In spite, however, of this better balance in training, modern medicine is very divided in its attitude to the new knowledge. Many first-class minds in medicine still cling to a purely materialistic attitude and believe that physical causes will be discovered for emotional disorders and so re-establish the pre-eminence of the earlier approach. Psychiatry is in an early stage of development and many doctors remain very sceptical of the value of dynamic psychology in the treatment of disease.

It can be fairly stated that the physical aspects of the doctor's training are at a high level and will enable him to develop the qualities that he needs in the physical sphere. In the field of mental health, however, although the student is receiving increasing help and training every year, the full effects of this have not yet become apparent, and there remains much conflict and difference of opinion.

When we turn to the spiritual aspects of illness, it is certainly true that no official place is given in medical training to the preparing of the doctor for the many problems with which he will be faced in his daily work. Certainly his patients will present him with spiritual issues. We are still faced with many baffling problems of incurable illness, death is a reality with which the doctor is constantly confronted, and his patients in their helplessness and the lonely business of suffering, look to him for help, support, guidance, and hope. Medical training fails the doctor here. Medicine alone has no message of hope for the incurable and the dying. The doctor will be consulted frequently on moral issues, will meet with resentment, bitterness and states of despair and despondency, and for none of these situations is medical training enough.

These facts lead to certain very important generalizations when we consider the doctor's probable attitude to spiritual healing. Firstly, the whole trend of his training tends to prejudice him against any non-physical method of healing and even many doctors of strong religious conviction find this prejudice extremely hard to overcome. Secondly, whilst there is a rapidly increasing awareness of the effect of emotional factors on the body, this knowledge is still too new and incomplete effectively to combat the prejudice already mentioned, although it is beginning to influence many to consider more seriously the claim of religion to play an important part in the business of healing. Lastly, the absence of any positive guidance about the spiritual problems of his patients tends, if he has no religious faith, to reinforce his defences against a spiritual approach in order to ward off feelings of anxiety and inadequacy. Thus many doctors adhere rigidly to the familiar role of physical healer, considering the spiritual problems entirely a matter for the minister of religion.

Apart from the more general aspects of medical training which help to determine the doctor's attitude to spiritual healing, there are certain more specific questions to be considered. On the whole doctors are extremely sceptical about the claims of cures made by those who practise various forms of religious healing. In itself this scepticism is a very healthy thing, because so many fantastic claims have been made. This attitude again grows out of the doctor's training. From the very beginning of his clinical work he is taught that, whenever possible, accurate diagnosis must precede treatment. Diagnosis is based upon careful history-taking, skilled examination, and clinical experience, supported by a variety of special investigations where appropriate. The doctor is understandably sceptical of any claims to healing that omit this vital assessment of the case. It is precisely in this matter of diagnosis that so much that is written and claimed by spiritual healing falls so sadly short. Religious healing can expect little sympathy and respect from the doctors unless it is prepared to be as exacting in its demands for accurate assessment as the medical profession. In works on healing frequent claims are made for the cure of cancer through prayer. These claims can only satisfy the doctor if they are backed up by accurate diagnosis, including microscopic section of the tumour, which alone establishes the diagnosis beyond doubt. The doctor cannot of course say that all these claims are false, but his training will rightly cause him to remain very cautious unless there is more convincing evidence of diagnosis than is usually provided.

Another problem which makes the acceptance of a spiritual approach difficult for the doctor is his attitude to incurable disease. Throughout his training he has been taught, and his experience has confirmed, that certain diseases are beyond question incurable in the present state of our knowledge, and others are relatively so. This teaching and experience makes him very careful in what he says to his patients and their relatives in many circumstances. He becomes very conscious of the hope and faith they place in him, and he dare not arouse false hopes only to see them shattered and his patient's suffering thereby increased. It appears to him that many who practice spiritual healing arouse false hope and misplaced faith, which in the long run can do nothing but harm, and are likely to cause much unnecessary suffering. With such people he does not feel he can co-operate, partly because his knowledge and training recoil from such an approach, and partly because of his loyalty to and concern for his patients. This problem of incurable disease also makes it much more difficult for the doctor than for others to take an active part in more responsible approaches to spiritual healing. He realizes that faith and the expectation that God will heal are basic attitudes in the religious approach, but his experience that certain diseases are incurable is so deeply ingrained in him that faith is doubly difficult to attain.

Whether or not he is himself a research worker, every doctor has been taught the basis upon which any sound and meaningful research work is done. Before any treatment can establish itself as of undoubted value, it is normally subjected to extensive and carefully controlled trials. Its apparent effectiveness in a few cases cannot be accepted as generally valid, since in any given situation so many factors are at work that no one can say with any assurance which is the effective one. In order to demonstrate beyond reasonable doubt that a new treatment really works, a very large series of cases must be treated and the results compared with a control group, carefully matched in as many particulars as possible but not receiving the new treatment. Such experiments demand time and patience and, equally important, an open mind. Because medical research is so objective and demanding, the doctor tends to be critical of the results of spiritual healing so far published. Too few cases have been reported, the work has been quite uncontrolled, and there has usually been little evidence of openmindedness. A further complication is the fact that it has long been known that certain diseases occasionally remit spontaneously, and therefore only a large series of cures would carry any conviction with the doctors. It is certainly open to question whether controlled experiments would ever be possible in the realm of spiritual healing, but it is important, if understanding is to be fostered, that the reasons for the doctor's critical attitude should be understood. He is, of course, as subject to prejudice as anyone else, but the fact of the matter is that all his training and experience demand that he should be severely critical. It is through the clearer understanding of these aspects of the doctor's training and attitudes that real progress will be made in the present encouraging tendency of medical men and ministers of religion to join together in the discussion of a combined approach to the practice of healing.

Stress has first been laid in this essay on those aspects of the doctor's approach to healing which make him cautious or create misunderstanding when he considers the question of spiritual healing. This has been done deliberately because of their great importance and the need for a responsible caution in this sphere. It would, however, give a false impression of the true position if nothing more positive was offered. Important though the scientific approach to modern medicine may be, it is nevertheless true that, at its best, medicine is an art just as truly as it is a science. One of the great dangers of present-day scientific medicine arises from the tendency for more and more detailed specialization, with an increasing number of experts concentrating upon a relatively small fraction of the total field. In this process the personal, individual nature of each patient can easily be lost sight of, until he becomes of less importance than his disease. This danger threatens the specialist to a greater degree than the general practitioner, but the latter is faced with the problem increasingly, as the complex nature of early diagnosis and treatment so often makes it impossible for him to treat the patient himself in the home environment. His consulting room is in danger of becoming a sorting-office and the personal interest in the whole man is difficult to maintain. The high standard of medical practice in this country witnesses to the remarkable degree in which these dangers are being combated, but that they are very real and demand our constant awareness cannot be denied, especially in the work of our hospitals.

It is just those intangible and immeasurable factors in healing, such as faith, hope, confidence and peace of mind, which are in danger of being overlooked in the growing complexity of our profession, and it is these same factors that are increasingly coming to light as of major importance in the prevention and healing of disease. Every doctor knows from experience rather than experiment that the patient who gives up hope has seriously impaired his chances, or at least the speed of recovery. Faith in the doctor and in the efficacy of his treatment has always been recognized as of the greatest importance, and modern psychiatric research has shown clearly that anxiety and conflict in the mind have very definite effects upon the proper functions of the body and play their part in causing disease. These important factors in human experience cannot be measured or assessed scientifically in the sense that we can accurately measure the presence and degree of anaemia in the blood, but few doctors would deny the importance of their detection, and correction if possible, as part and parcel of the art of medical practice.

More and more evidence is accumulating that stress plays an important part in the etiology of most of our present-day diseases, and not only in the neuroses. The eradication in this country of many of the more obvious stress factors, such as poverty and material insecurity, has changed the pattern of disease rather than lessened the total sum of suffering due to illness. As the material conditions of life have improved, it has become increasingly clear that internal stress due to emotional conflict and its attendant anxiety is the greatest challenge in our approach to healing today.

It is doubtful if the real impact of this fact has yet been felt by the medical profession as a whole, and there is much resistance to its acceptance. This resistance is probably due to a number of factors. The physical bias in a doctor's training has already been mentioned, and to this must be added our relative lack of understanding of how to treat this aspect of disease even when it is recognized. Nevertheless, the growing awareness of the importance of emotional and spiritual factors in all disease and ill-health is clearly the common ground on which medicine and the Church can meet, in an attempt to hammer out a combined approach to prevention and treatment which takes account of the whole man, and which should play an important part in correcting the materialistic bias which medicine has acquired in the last century.

To Christian people, the need for full co-operation between the Church and the doctors is very plain in view of the factors reviewed in this essay. In practice, however, many difficulties arise which need to be clarified. Ministers of religion are not infrequently heard to complain that it is difficult to gain real co-operation from the doctor. Behind such complaints there would seem to be the tacit assumption that medicine is, or should be, based upon Christian principles and beliefs, but this is not so, and this fact needs to be clearly faced. The minister has strong convictions about the relevance of the Christian faith to the modern understanding of the etiology of disease, and in addition he accepts the authority of Christ that it is part of the Church's task to heal the sick; but a great many doctors have no compelling religious convictions, and whilst they may share some of the conventional ethics of Christianity, the idea of a living God who is active in the affairs of men, and through whom spiritual resources effective in healing can be tapped by faith, is utterly meaningless. Co-operation in the real sense of the word is only possible between people who share the same basic faith and conviction. This is not to say that no effective co-operation is possible with agnostic doctors, but it will issue from a practical demonstration of the effectiveness of a Christian approach to healing rather than from a shared conviction. The Church as a whole is very far at present from presenting any effective demonstration of the power for healing which it claims, but where this does exist, there is at least a basis for co-operation which might lead in time to real conviction in some of those doctors who at present have no real religious faith. It is in this sense that the effective ministry of healing could at the same time be effective evangelization.

Real co-operation, that is to say a positive Christian approach from both sides working together, has already begun, and there are many groups of doctors and ministers of religion meeting together to deepen their understanding of the problem and to learn how best they can work together. Even in these circumstances problems still remain. Perhaps the most important is the lack of knowledge and training on both sides about how to approach the emotional problems of disease. A great deal of knowledge has now accumulated about them, and the doctor rightly feels that, however incomplete his own physical approach may be, any non-physical approach to healing should take full account of such facts as are known. Considering the Christian Ministry as a whole, in all its denominations, it is still largely true that no effective training is given in our theological colleges to prepare a minister for dealing with the many emotional problems manifest in personal relationships which are evidence of the conflicts underlying so much ill-health. There are encouraging signs that the demand is growing for such training and that those responsible for planning the curriculum of theological students are studying the possibilities. It would, however, be unfair to suggest that the lack in training lies on one side only. Much still needs to be done in medical education before it can be claimed that the majority of doctors have any real understanding of the complexity of the emotional factors in stress diseases or any effective skill in treating them beyond an intuitive sympathy with the weakness of human nature. Much time and planning is needed before these things can be accomplished but they are being increasingly tackled.

Lastly, ministers, Christian doctors and laymen are all sadly aware of the gap between formal Christian practice evidenced in Church membership together with a certain ethical standard of behaviour, and a real demonstration in their daily living and personal relationships of the effectiveness of the Christian Gospel of love which in New Testament times was so productive of healing. Here is perhaps the most uncontroversial, and in the long run most effective meeting point of Christians, both doctors and ministers, in the task of co-operating in the healing of the sick. It is from the really effective fellowship of the local Church that doctors, ministers and laymen should go out equipped with a living faith which will be woven into the pattern of all that makes up their personal and professional lives, and give new life and effect to their particular professional skills.

10
Co-operation of Minister and Doctor
Lewis H. Allison and R. Paxton Graham

CO-OPERATION OF MINISTER AND DOCTOR

'My son, in thy sickness be not negligent; but pray unto the Lord, and He will make thee whole. Leave off from sin, and order thine own hands aright, and cleanse thy heart from all wickedness. . . . Then give place to the physician, for the Lord hath created him; Let him not go from thee, for thou hast need of him.'

Ecclesiasticus 38$^{9-10,\ 12}$

INTRODUCTION

IT HAS BEEN said that in the nineteenth century the interests of a Yorkshire village centred in the church, the local inn, and the cricket club. Each of the three, however, possessed its own character, and whilst villagers might support each in its turn, there was no confusion in the minds of the people concerning them, for each had its own place and its own time. Like the sides of a triangle they only touched at the points where they diverged.

In like manner, in English life, the doctor and the minister have been well-honoured figures, the relationship between them, in the popular mind, consisting of the supposed fact that the one carried on where the other left off. In the Church's history the two groups have gradually become separated; the New Testament commandment, 'Preach, saying, The kingdom of heaven is at hand. Heal the sick, raise the dead, cleanse the lepers, cast out devils' (Mt 10$^{7-8}$), has been complied with mainly by the ministers concentrating on the first half and the doctors on the second half. The problem before us, therefore, is to bring the two professions once more into a unity. This will not mean that both will do the same work, but that each of their duties will be regarded as only a part of an indivisible whole, one being the complement of the other. In order to do this both doctor and minister must have a full understanding of the function of the other as seen, not only from his own point of view, but also from 'the other side of the fence'.

The history of non-medical interest in healing is dealt with in another chapter. What we are concerned with here is not only what Phyllis Garlick has called 'a renewal of partnership',[1] but also the roles of each professional in the context of modern dynamic theories. Christianity has always sought to relieve pain and suffering, for as von Hügel has said, 'Christianity has taught us to care'. Not until this generation, however, has the Christian Church, or indeed the medical profession, understood with such deep insight the biblical conception of man's wholeness. Yet an individual is not an isolated 'whole', living *in vacuo*; he lives in a community, in a family, with political and religious systems to which he owes allegiance more or less strongly. This has been expressed by Paul Tillich: 'No individual exists without participation, and no personal being exists without communal being.'[2] An individual who is ill, or un-whole-some, has special needs requiring the ministrations of others, amongst whom are essentially the doctor and the minister. This modern dynamic approach is the result of several approaches or strands coming together from very different sources.

The first of these is presented to us, strangely, by one who confessedly was no friend of religion, the Viennese neurologist, Sigmund Freud. As a genuine scientist, Freud put us all in his debt by supplying a key by which the mysteries of much abnormal behaviour might be opened up; he made us aware of the unconscious mind. Into the unconscious, unwelcome thoughts and disturbing emotions are repressed, producing tension and anxiety. Here was common ground upon which doctor and minister could wander without either of them being accused of trespassing directly upon the territory of the other. That here lie hidden pits into which the unwary, untutored and inexperienced may fall, sending into a deeper mire those they would help, calls insistently for a caveat. Yet there is here in the realm of the affects, or emotions, an overlapping of the fields of medicine and the Church, which demands an awareness of conditions transcending the narrower borders of any single profession or discipline. Thus the doctor in his function as a healer may have to concern himself with the 'spiritual' condition of his patient, apparently trespassing into the realm once regarded as sacrosanct to the minister. Nor need the minister feel that 'religion' has failed him when he recommends a mentally disturbed member to a doctor or psychiatrist. In this

[1] *Health and Healing.*
[2] *Systematic Theology.*

field of the emotions both doctor and minister work with a single purpose, the well-being of the patient.

The second strand comes from the philosophical side where the controversies of the eighteenth and nineteenth centuries over the 'body-mind' relationship are resolved by, at least, a sort of working agreement. Christian belief holds, claims E. L. Mascall, that a human being is not a pure spirit temporarily inhabiting a material segment, but a psychophysical unity in which body and soul are intimately and mysteriously locked.[3] In this unitary concept that man is not a body *and* a mind, but a 'body-mind', that there is no mind without a body and no living body without a mind, the theories of Spinoza's Parallelism, Huxley's Epiphenomenalism and Christianity's Interactionism are each resolved by a working basis acceptable to each and offending none.[4] No longer need man be torn asunder for the sake of theoretical simplicity: he is a 'body-mind', a psychophysical unity, whose health depends upon his wholeness.

The third strand comes from sociology. Man belongs to a community to whose influences he reacts and in which there is a fairly thorough two-way traffic. We know that at any given moment a man's moral behaviour, as well as his physical condition, is determined in no small degree by his social background and environment. In his essay in 'The Church and Mental Health' (Ed. Paul B. Maves), Seward Hiltner claims that the sciences of man have made impossible a dialectic or fragmented approach to health and illness; the body and the mind, the emotions and the spirit, and the interpersonal relationships, are all involved and at all times. Social psychologists are adamant in affirmation that neither the materialistic nor the spiritualistic types can be understood without examining man's environment, especially that aspect of it which is closest to him as a person, namely his relationship with other people. Emphasis on the importance of these sociological influences has also been given by the neo-Freudian schools of Karen Horney and Erich Fromm. The presence of almoners in our hospitals is a recognition of this fact as it affects the health of the patients. Emotional maturity and inner confidence arising out of right relationships are requirements of all who would be made whole. Here the doctor and the minister are reminded that in the interests

[3] *Christian Theology and Natural Science.*
[4] For further discussion see *The Concepts of the Mind*, G. Ryle (1949), and *The Neurophysiological Basis of Mind*, J. C. Eccles (1953).

of the patient they must team up together with other social workers.

The fourth strand, and not the least, is that of religion. The structure of society in this country, whether it is liked and agreed with or not, has a background of religion woven into life's pattern, and the warp and weft require an adjustment one way or another to this theological interpretation of life. In a preface to a work on the philosopher Nietzsche, Dr Oscar Levy, a staunch opponent of Christianity, admitted it to be 'a mighty religion still, a religion which has governed the world for 2,000 years, which has influenced all philosophies, all literatures, all laws, all customs up to our present day, till it has finally filtered into our hearts, our blood, our system, and become part and parcel of ourselves without our being aware of it. At the present time we are all instinctive Christians.' These are strong words, but who can gainsay their truth? Confirmation is further provided, and the implication clearly revealed, by C. G. Jung.[5] Going carefully over his records for thirty years Jung discovered that the mental disorders of his mature patients were traceable to some loss of religious faith, and that restoration to health was dependent upon the recovery of a new and stronger religious conviction.

The dilemma confronting man, to be resolved only by faith, has been poignantly put by W. H. V. Reade: 'It makes not the slightest difference whether matter is as hard as adamant, as stodgy as suet, as volatile as gas, as agile as electricity, or as naked as mathematical formula. The only relevant question is whether it is self-existent or created by God.'[6] If we hold, as indeed we do, that this is God's world, created and sustained by Him, then we must make our adjustment to Him and His world if a state of well-being is to be enjoyed and we are to be in a state of health. Jesus affirmed the essential part of faith in healing when He said to one, 'Thy sins be forgiven thee', and to another, 'Thy faith hath made thee whole'.

The doctor's duty to the world is said to be to maintain men in, or to restore them to, a state of complete health or wholeness. Such a statement depends on the definition of 'complete health or wholeness' given by the World Health Organization in 1947, which defined health as a 'complete state of physical, mental, and social well-being'. As Christians we would add to this definition:

[5] *Modern Man in Search of a Soul.*
[6] *The Christian Challenge to Philosophy.*

CO-OPERATION OF MINISTER AND DOCTOR

'spiritual well-being.' An important feature of this wider definition is that to the modern mind health is not merely an absence of disease, but something dynamic, a positive progressive force. If then the maintenance, restoration or encouragement of this kind of health be our aim, it will be apparent how enormous is the task and how essential it is for all professionals concerned to learn to work together.

IS CO-OPERATION DESIRED AND TO WHAT EXTENT IS IT PRACTISED?

We ask first of all, desired by whom? Three parties, at least, are involved; the doctor, the minister and the patient. We must not forget the patient, for as student-nurses are taught, the most important person in a hospital ward is the patient. But what of the doctors and ministers in general practice? To what extent is co-operation being carried out in the country? In order to ascertain some facts a questionnaire was prepared and sent out to 205 ministers; they were mostly Methodists but a few were Anglicans. This was the questionnaire:

(1) How many times have you made an approach to a doctor on behalf of any of your people in the ordinary course of your pastoral work during (a) the past year? . . . (b) the past three years? . . .
(2) How many times has a doctor approached you with regard to one of his patients during (a) the past year? . . . (b) the past three years? . . .
(3) What were the natures of the 'troubles' for which the approaches were made? Place the number against the appropriate designation. (a) medical . . . (b) domestic and social . . . . (c) mental . . . (d) religious and ethical . . . (e) any others. . . .
(4) Bearing in mind that in 1947 the Council of the B.M.A. recorded no ethical reason why medical practitioners should not co-operate with clergy, would you personally welcome, and to what degree, co-operation between doctor and minister as it relates to your own work? Please answer by using the following five-point scale. (i) Definitely No . . . (ii) Would prefer not . . . (iii) Indifferent . . . (iv) Prepared to if necessary (v) Definitely Yes. . . .

(5) What in your opinion are the main obstacles to further co-operation? ....
(6) Any further observations or comments you think may be helpful in this inquiry ....

The questionnaires were sent to Methodist ministers in the industrial area of Durham County, the industrial and rural areas of Northumberland, a mainly rural area in the South, and to Methodist ministers and Anglican clergy in a North-east town. 125 replies were received from the 205 questionnaires sent out, a higher ratio than is usually expected from inquiries of this sort.

Over a period of three years each minister approached doctors on average in 1·39 cases, or in firm figures 4 cases in 9 years. Each doctor approached ministers in ·66 cases on average in three years, or in firm figures 2 cases in 9 years. 94 ministers said 'Definitely Yes' to co-operation, 30 were prepared to co-operate if necessary, and only one (an Anglican) claimed to be indifferent. None was opposed.

The largest number of approaches made were on account of mental disorders; medical matters were a good second; social and domestic affairs came a good third; and only 22 approaches out of 256 were on account of religious and ethical matters. A total of 159 reasons were offered to account for the difficulty in co-operation. These could be reduced to a few main ones, the more insistent being (a) pressure of work on both sides, (b) the agnosticism of many doctors, (c) lack of knowledge and training on the part of ministers, (d) professional isolation.

Two points stood out very clearly: first, the expressed willingness of ministers to co-operate (75 per cent said they were very keen, and not a single reason was offered in opposition); second, the negligible amount reported as being done. As an addendum to this there was noted the insignificant recognition given to ethical and spiritual troubles. If the present survey is indicative of doctor-minister co-operation throughout the country, it is clear that at present co-operation is rather an idealized dream talked about by the few than a realized fact acted upon by the many.

REQUIREMENTS FOR THE INTEGRATION OF EFFORT

A beginning may be made by recognizing that the large majority of both ministers and doctors are 'general practitioners'. They are in direct contact with the community in health and sickness. They are never off duty, for they are dealing with the community as a community and as individuals in a general way all the time. It is important that the doctor and the minister should keep the fact before them that they are 'general practitioners' and not specialists. How easy it is for a young minister to work hard in his youth club and overlook the necessity for an adequate amount of time to be given to pastoral work amongst older members with their mental, moral, and spiritual needs! And how easy it is for the doctor who excels in midwifery to dismiss his neurotic patients with the prescription of 'rest and a tonic'!

In the approaches of doctor and minister there are, of course, important distinctions. It is said broadly and popularly that the approach of the minister will be from a spiritual and ethical angle, and that of the doctor from a psychosomatic angle. This must not be taken to mean that man is divided into two entities, as though he were a machine inhabited by a spirit or angel. Though it be acknowledged that man possesses a spiritual aspect, this does not deny that instinctive tendencies are active in him or that mental experiences are related to and dependent upon his physical senses —*nihil in intellectu quod non prius in sensu*. Successful co-operation between the doctor and the minister depends upon a certain synthesis, but before this can be achieved it will be necessary to consider the aims of the minister, *qua* minister, and the doctor, *qua* doctor, in order to evaluate the kind of help each can offer to the other.

Amongst his other important duties, the minister possesses a 'Pastoral' function; He who called Himself the 'Good Shepherd' commanded: 'Feed my sheep.' This involves a personal concern for individuals, recalling that two of the greatest recorded discourses of our Lord were delivered to congregations of one, namely, to Nicodemus and to the Samaritan Woman. Most people in distress or in need of guidance turn first either to their local doctor or minister. The minister is approached with a variety of matters concerning employment, marriage, money, legal affairs, education, domestic difficulties, morals, Scripture interpretation, prayer and much else. In all these things he is to his people a friend, a teacher and a guide, working at conscious level; he relieves anxieties partly by imparting information.

The minister knows, however, that many of the problems brought to him go deeper and lie below the surface. In these matters he will need to do more than give advice, for he will be dealing with wrong attitudes and faulty relationships. Disturbances of these deeper things will require the minister to do more listening than talking, and for him to bring about a new understanding rather than to offer counsel. For this kind of work he will need special preparation and training, and a readiness to learn by experience. In meeting these tensions he will often be able, within his pastoral office, to fulfil a function that is preventive of more serious disturbance, though it be by a sort of 'first-aid' treatment.

Not infrequently the minister meets with emotional disorders of a more intransigent character requiring specialist knowledge. Although a few ministers may have received the training appropriate to help these cases in conjunction with a doctor, it is unlikely that more than a very few will ever have this training, and even fewer will have the time needed to deal adequately with those requiring this deeper analytic help. It is not the function of the minister to practise psychotherapy, though his work as a pastor may have and indeed should have therapeutic value.

The time has now about passed when the medical profession was divided on the question of psychology. Much water has flowed under the bridge of medicine since the days of 1914–18 when Rivers, Brown, McDougal, Crichton Miller, Hadfield and others blazoned the psychological trail in medicine. Nevertheless the new methods in psychiatry which are proving so successful must not lead us to disparage pathological research, for instance on the viruses, because it deals with the organism 'in parts' and not 'as a whole'. The general practitioner, however, must see illness as a dysfunction of the total personality. This will lead him to take account not only of the latest drugs from chemical research and the latest treatment by physical methods in the hospitals, but also of the work of the Church and the various social organizations. In the hospital the doctor under whose charge a patient is placed will need the help of many others—the nursing staff, the radiologist, the physiotherapist, and so on. He does not think of them as fulfilling a lower role, but as doing that for which they are especially equipped. So too the doctor in general practice will see in the minister and the social worker those who have been equipped along their own lines to take an appropriate part in the process of making man whole.

WAYS OF ACHIEVEMENT

No co-operation is possible until both doctor and minister recognize the validity of the approach of the other; barriers due to misunderstandings easily arouse doubts. One of these is the difference in language spoken; professional terms are a middle wall of partition, for they constitute a sort of secret code which can be deciphered only by those initiated by professional training. Much may be done to break down this barrier by members of the two professions meeting. The bona fides of each will be best appreciated when they meet as personal friends and talk informally, and when groups of ministers and doctors meet in a local fellowship in the way encouraged by the Methodist Society for Medical and Pastoral Psychology, in which members of both professions can be introduced to the ways of medico-pastoral work.

In an essay entitled 'The Parish Minister and the Psychiatrist in Co-operation and Contrast' (ed. Paul V. Kaves op. cit.), Dallas Pratt has suggested that the minister might learn from the roles of the various workers in the Psychiatric Clinic. Team work is increasingly coming to the fore, a fact to be learned by doctors and ministers alike. In this country Child Guidance Clinics are very willing for observers to sit in at the weekly conference of psychiatrist, psychologist, paediatrician, social worker, and education officer. From such examples of team work in even one particular sphere he would be dull indeed who did not see how he as doctor or minister could fit into work of a corporate character such as Parents and Community Associations, etc.

Health problems of the community such as in slum clearance, V.D., drug addiction, alcoholism and prostitution are both ethical and medical matters, and should be considered by minister and doctor together. To meet this need the two professions might establish local and national councils of social health, submitting their recommendations to local authorities and parliament. A good example of this in practice is the Marriage Guidance Council. An extension into other fruitful fields where integration is required, such as the law and social work generally, needs urgent consideration.

The propagation of positive health and the intelligent understanding of disease is the responsibility of both professions, and in the future the most productive field of co-operation may well lie not in the cure of disease but in its prevention. The parable of

'Lifeboats and Lighthouses' suggested by Graham Ikin is appropriate, the former being called out in crises, the latter being built to prevent them, and reminding us of the words of our Lord: 'I am the Light of the World.' This has been stressed succinctly by W. R. Fairbairn, who claims that the most important contribution of psychoanalysis to the cause of mental health lies in the preventive rather than the therapeutic field.[7] In the application of psychoanalytic principles to the upbringing of children lies the chief hope, he thinks. We must, therefore, turn to the task of enlightening the general public, parents and educators, about the emotional needs, conflicts, and deprivations of the child. In the cause of making men whole this applies to others as well as to children, and to maladies other than emotional ones.

Doctor and minister might usefully share the same platform in advocacy of community interests. The togetherness of both will itself help people to associate in their minds the work of medicine and that of the Church. It will do more. At present, insufficient emphasis is laid upon the voluntary and semi-voluntary social services. But for the work done by Moral Welfare committees, Family Service Units, Guilds of Help, Meals on Wheels, Marriage Guidance Councils, and many others, the amount of suffering in the country would be greatly increased. These organizations are immensely helped as they are served and advocated jointly by doctor and minister. If, with the minister and doctor, other workers in industry, child welfare and education could be teamed up, utilizing the wealth of experience and information of them all, the aim of providing a healthy environment for healthy people would be brought nearer.[8]

There is a place also for the joint working of minister and doctor within the Church, endeavouring to bring the laity within the scope of the healing ministry. One of the writers of this essay has experimented by holding in his house a monthly meeting of Church members with the minister as well as the doctor in attendance. The group first resolves itself into a prayer cell of intercession for the sick of the Church and others outside the Church known to the group or members of the group. Discussion follows about practical ways of helping—e.g. house cleaning,

---

[7] *B.J.M.P.* (June 1957).
[8] *Parsons Meet Welfare Workers*, the story of the British Council of Churches' Conference at Mottram Hall, ed. Harold Lees, gives an example of a line to be further pursued.

nursing, helping with the children, buying extra comforts and generally doing whatever will relieve tension and enable the needy person or family to make a successful recovery or readjustment. This follows on the practical side something of the kind of work undertaken by the Family Service Units, except that it is done on an entirely voluntary basis and on the more definite foundation of Christian fellowship and prayer. Whilst the F.S.U. utilizes trained case-workers, in the above experiment the ordinary Church member is encouraged to realize that he as well as the 'specialist' is a part of the Church's healing ministry. This surely is in accordance with the mind of our Lord: 'I am come that they might have life, and that they might have it more abundantly.'

INDEX

(References to Proper Names printed in Capitals)

A
ADLER, 65, 153
AERIUS, 22
ALCMAEON, 12
Anxiety, 130
AQUINAS, Thomas, 120
ASA, 6
ASCLEPIUS, 10
Assyria, 3
AUGUSTINE, 24, 25, 93

B
Babylonia, 3
BARNES, G. O., 29
BASIL, 3
BEERS, C. W., 60
BENEDICT, 25
BERNADETTE, 39
Body-Mind Relationship, 171
Brain, the, 127
BRIGHT, John, 29

C
Cancer, 163
Catharsis, 143
CELSUS, 16
CHAD, 25
Chakrams, 45
CHARDIN de, 111
Child Guidance Clinics, 177
Christian Science, 38
Clairvoyance, 43, 50
Confession, 59, 142
COUÉ, 28, 31, 34
Counselling, 155
CYPRIAN, 20

D
Dark Night of the Soul, 149
DAY, Sir George, 40
Death, 151
Demonology, 74, 85
Depth Psychology, 153
Diagnosis, 163
DIGBY, Sir Kenelm, 27
Distraction, 146
Dowsers, 46
Dryness in Prayer, 148

E
EDDY, Mrs, 38
EDWARDS, Harry, 41, 46
ELISHA, 6
'Empathy', 150
EPHREM the SYRIAN, 24
Epidaurus, 10, 11
Epiphenomenalism, 171
ERASISTRATUS, 15
Evil, problem of, 93, 96
Exorcism, 20

F
Faith, 56, 73, 79, 116
FAIRBAIRN, W. F., 178
Fall, The, 93, 96
FAVERCHES, Richeldis de, 25
FLEW, Anthony, 95
Forgiveness, 144
Free Will, 93, 95
FREUD, 65, 153, 170
FROMM, Erich, 171

G

GALEN, 16
GARBETT, Dr, 52
GARLICK, Phyllis, 170
GASSNER, S. S., 28
GOSSE, Edmond, 28
GREATRAKES, Valentine, 27
Greeks and disease, 7
GREGORY, Thaumaturgos, 22
GREGORY of TOURS, 24
Guilt and Sickness, 84, 143

H

HADFIELD, Dr J. A., 63, 64, 176
HAMMURABI, 5
Heat, 46
Hebrew theory of disease, 5
HELL, Maximilian, 27
HEROPHILUS, 15
HILDEGARD of BINGEN, 26
HILTNER, Seward, 171
HIPPOCRATES, 12, 31
HIPPOLYTUS, Canons of, 20
HODGES, H. A., 149
Holy Communion, 20, 145
HORNEY, Karen, 171
HOWARD, John, 28
HÜGEL VON, 170
HUGH of LINCOLN, 25
HUXLEY, 171
Hypnotism, 36, 121
Hysteria, 130

I

IKIN, Graham, 178
'Iliad', 8
Incarnation, The, 73, 98
Incubation, 10, 20
Incurable Disease, 163
Inheritance, 128
Interactionism, 171
Intercession for the Sick, 57, 103, 107
Interviewing, 155

Ionic thinkers, 11

J

JEROME, 24
JUNG, 11, 62, 68, 153, 172
JUSTIN MARTYR, 22

K

King's Touch, 26

L

Lachish, 6
LAW, William, 146
Laying on of hands, 20, 55, 99
LEVY, Oscar, 172
Lourdes, 10, 39, 51

M

Magic, 2, 6
Magnetism, 27, 28, 34f, 43
MAILLARD, John, 57
MANDUS, Brother, 46
Marriage Guidance Council, 177, 178
MASCALL, E. L., 171
Masturbation, 62
MÉDARD, St., 28
Medical training, 160
Medicine today, 164
Meditation, 146
MESMER, 27, 34
Miracle, 71, 75, 92, 104, 114, 120
Missions, Healing, 50
MONTFORT, Simon de, 25

N

Name-Magic, 23
Natural Law, 104, 118
'Nephesh', 7
Neurosis, 154, 161
NEWMAN, J. H., 28
NICEPHORUS, 24

O

Odic Force, 28, 42, 57

Odyssey, 9
ORIGEN, 23

P
PARACELSUS, 27
Parallelism, 17
PEYRAMALE, 40
PLATO, 15
PRATT, Dallas, 177
Prayer, 108, 113, 146
Prayer Fellowship, 152
Psychiatric Clinic, 177
Psychiatry among the Greeks, 15
Psychiatry and the Minister, 63
Psychoanalysis, 178
Psychometry, 50
Psychosis, 134, 154

Q
Quakers, 27

R
Radiaesthesia, 27, 32, 42, 49
READE, W. H. V., 172
REICHENBACH, Karl von, 43
Relics, 24
Repressions, 130
ROSE, Dr Louis, 42
'Ruach', 7

S
Sacramentary of Serapion, 21
Saints, healings by, 23
SALMON, Mrs, 46
Serpent Symbol, 11
Shepherd of Hermas, 20
SHORNE, Sir John, 25
Shrines, 25
Sin, 143, 148
Skin disease, 67, 75, 127

Sociology, 171
SPINOZA, 171
Spiritual direction, 142
Spiritual healing, 99
Spiritualism and healing, 48, 49
STREETER, 92
Stress, 165
Suffering, reality of, 94
Suggestions, auto, 34
Suggestibility, 51
Superego, 130, 131

T
TELLING, Maxwell, 64
Temperament, 129
TENNANT, F. R., 94
Theology and Healing, 91
TILLICH, Paul, 117, 141, 170
TRUDEL, Dorothea, 29
Tuberculosis, 47, 49

U
Unction, 21, 46, 57, 77

V
Visitation of the Sick, 150

W
WELLS, 25
WESLEY, John, 28, 149
WILLIAMS, Tennessee, 115
WILSON, Jim, 57
WOODS, Dr, Bishop of Lichfield, 48
WORDSWORTH, William, 118
World Health Organization, 172
WYCLIFF, John, 114

Y
YELLOWLEES, Dr David, 62

www.ingramcontent.com/pod-product-compliance
Lightning Source LLC
Chambersburg PA
CBHW071449150426
43191CB00008B/1286